Lecture Notes in Economics and Mathematical Systems

Operations Research, Computer Science, Social Science

Edited by M. Beckmann, Providence, G. Goos, Karlsruhe, and H. P. Künzi, Zürich

70

J. P. Brown

The Economic Effects of Floods

Investigations of a Stochastic Model of Rational Investment Behavior in the Face of Floods

Springer-Verlag
Berlin · Heidelberg · New York 1972

Prof. John P. Brown
Brown University
Dept. of Economics
Providence, R. I. 02912/USA

AMS Subject Classifications (1970): 90 A 05

ISBN 3-540-05925-3 Springer-Verlag Berlin · Heidelberg · New York
ISBN 0-387-05925-3 Springer-Verlag New York · Heidelberg · Berlin

Offsetdruck: Julius Beltz, Hemsbach/Bergstr.

PREFACE

This monograph is a revised version of the author's doctoral dissertation for the Economics Department of the University of California, Berkeley, 1970. It is a summary and extension of work done by a group of people in Berkeley from 1966 to 1969. They are Professor C. B. McGuire, formerly at the School of Business Administration at Berkeley and now at the Graduate School of Public Affairs there, who directed the work of the group and the dissertation, Professor Bruno Contini at the time a lecturer in the School of Business Administration and now at the University of Torino, Italy, and Manish Bhattacharjee, formerly a graduate student at Berkeley and now at the Indian Institute of Management, Calcutta. We worked very closely together, so it is very difficult to trace the provenance of any of the particular ideas presented here. However, the major outlines of the study were developed jointly by McGuire, Contini, and myself and were recently published (see Brown, Contini, and McGuire, 1972). The technical aspects of the dynamic programming in the study were much advanced by Bhattacharjee. His contributions are largely contained in his working paper (see Bhattacharjee, 1968). Thus the credit for any useful output must be shared, but the responsibility for any errors is my own.

The work of Brown, Contini and McGuire in 1966 and 1967 was financed by the U.S. Army Corps of Engineers and the work of McGuire, Brown, and Bhattarcharjee from 1967 to 1969 was financed by the Department of the Interior, Office of Water Resources Research. For this support we are extremely grateful. It should be noted that views expressed here are those of the author and not necessarily those of the supporting agencies.

I would like to thank Marion Anthony who typed the manuscript so expertly. Finally, I want to thank my wife, Mary, who helped in countless ways.

February, 1972
Providence, Rhode Island

TABLE OF CONTENTS

CHAPTER 1

INTRODUCTION

There is by now a large literature on the economic aspects of flood control and flood relief policies. The contribution of this paper lies in its careful scrutiny of one single critical aspect of the economics of floods, the choice of land use by a single landowner. We analyze that choice using the methods of dynamic programming, and in particular, we show how that choice is dependent on the probability of floods for his piece of land. The theory we have developed here has been developed in the context of floods. In fact, this work grew out of an empirical study of flood plain damages, when we found that the underlying theory was not yet developed.[1]

In fact, we feel that the theory is of much more general interest. It is a theory of optimal investment choice under uncertainty when that uncertainty is a result of destruction or failure of the investment at a random date. This is the case in flood plains, but it is also the appropriate basic theory for understanding investment decisions in the face of earthquakes, fires, war damage, avalanches, and other kinds of disasters. These are only the more dramatic examples of situations where replacement is required at an uncertain date.

By concentrating on the rational decisions of individuals we develop a theory to explain how individuals will respond to a variety of government policies which either change the probability of floods, e.g., a dam or levee, or change the costs of replacement of activities after a flood such as flood victim relief measures. We can also show the impact of the availability of flood insurance on choices of activity.

The verification of the descriptive value of the model remains to be carried out. The prescriptive value is evident, however, As with most applications of dynamic programming we have a realized proscriptive tool and a potential descriptive tool.

---

[1]See U.S. Army Corps of Engineers, 1967.

Outline of the Study

Chapter Two is devoted to making the simplifying assumptions necessary to fit the problem into a very simple dynamic programming framework. First, we assume that the investor (or landowner or decision maker, we use these terms interchangeably) can be described by an intertemporal analogue of the Von Neumann-Morgenstern utility function, and we discuss the implications of that assumption. Then we go on to assume that the available mutually exclusive investment activities are sufficiently well understood and well behaved that they can be completely described by the stream of payments that they generate over time. Some minor complications are introduced when we address the problem of choosing when to replace an investment, even without regard to floods.

Floods are very complicated phenomena, with no two exactly alike. Obviously we must simplify both the effects of floods and the probability structure of flooding in order to fit them into a manageable framework. This we do by assuming that floods destroy everything and that they are generated by a simple stochastic process, the Poisson process. Then we go on to discuss why these assumptions are more robust than they appear. We also appeal to the authority of hydrologists and their practices.

That done we can go on in Chapter 3 to develop the dynamic programming model and show how the landowner will identify the best of the available investment strategies. Because of the simplifying assumptions made in Chapter 2 the solution is a very simple exercise. Because of the recurrence built into the problem, that investment activity which is optimal today will be optimal at any date. Once we find the best activity for the first interflood interval we can be assured that it will always be the best.

Chapter 4 rephrases the problem in an optimal replacement framework. This has the advantage of allowing us to solve for the optimal replacement interval as part of a larger optimizing problem. It also gives us a better insight into the problem, since we can view the effect of a flood as forcing the investor to replace the incumbent activity at a suboptimal date.

Chapter 5 leads us into a much more difficult area. Here we drop the assumption that the probability of floods is known. Instead we follow the so-called Bayesian approach and assume that the landowner has beliefs about the true value of the unknown flood parameter which can be described by a subjective probability distribution. As he learns more by observing the flood plain through the years he adjusts this probability distribution in such a way that it will get tighter around the true value of the parameter. This is simpler to analyze if we assume that the probability distributions which describe his beliefs, both before and after observations, are members of an easily described family of distributions called conjugate families of distributions. For our problem the appropriate conjugate family is the gamma-1 distribution family which is described by two parameters corresponding to the length of an observation and the number of floods observed.

Even in the simplest case, the case where investment decisions are made only immediately after a flood, the problem is so complicated that we cannot simply calculate the optimal program. Instead we suggest some bounds on the value of the optimal program and some approximations and simplifications to get around the problem. Then we go on to describe the structure of the problem when optimal replacement dates are known, a case of intermediate complexity, as well as when the decision-maker can change activities at any time, the optimal replacement case.

In Chapter 6 we turn to an elementary discussion of government policy when landowners behave as we have assumed in the earlier chapters. The analytical apparatus is much simpler here than in the earlier chapters and is much easier reading. Here we deal with the logical structure of evaluating a variety of government policies, dams, flood insurance, relief measures for flood victims, and flood plain zoning. For dams we show what should count toward the benefits of the dam, and for the rest we show the allocative or misallocative effects of various policies. Since much of the previous literature does not distinguish sufficiently carefully between the damages from floods and the benefits of flood prevention we start Chapter 6 with a discussion of flood damages and their relation to flood prevention benefits.

Chapter 7 describes a computer simulation program for simulation analysis of the Bayesian problem.

CHAPTER 2

BACKGROUND AND ASSUMPTIONS

The Landowner or Investor

We may express the investor's preferences in terms of expectations because we shall use the expected utility maximization hypothesis as the explanation of how the decision maker evaluates rewards. This hypothesis, developed by Ramsey and Von Neumann and Morgenstern, is now the standard approach used by economists and psychologists to problems of decision making under uncertainty.[1] With this approach, the individual's preferences are described in terms of a utility function which has gambles as arguments and which conforms to the probability calculus, so that the most preferred gamble is the one with the highest expected utility.

Before the investor's preferences can be described in such a convenient fashion, the following assumptions about them must be made:[2] (i) A weak preference ordering holds over all possible lottery prizes and it is transitive. (ii) Compound lotteries can be reduced to simple lotteries with the same prizes and appropriately calculated probabilities. (iii) If $A \geq B \geq C$, there is some probability p in the lottery $(p, A; (1-p), C)$ such that he is indifferent between the lottery and B (continuity). (iv) Indifferent prizes can be substituted into a lottery without changing the individual's evaluation of the lottery (substitutability). (v) Preference and indifference among lotteries are transitive relations. (vi) When $A > B$, a lottery $(p, A; (1-p)\ B)$ is preferred to the lottery $(r, A; (1-r)\ B)$ if and only if $p > r$. When these assumptions hold, the individual's preferences can be described by a utility function such that he behaves as if he were a maximizer of the expected value of utility.

---

[1]See Ramsey, 1926, Von Neumann and Morgenstern, 1947, for the classic original statements of the theory. Luce and Raiffa, 1957, present a clear modern discussion of the theory from the point of view of economists, while the readings in Edwards and Tversky, 1967, reflect more of the psychological point of view.

[2]See Luce and Raiffa, 1957, Chapter 2 for a complete discussion of these assumptions.

Because the landowner's decisions about his use of the land affect payment streams which extend into the future, we shall need a slight extension of the theory to include intertemporal choice. We shall assume that the individual discounts future utility at a constant rate, a standard assumption. Thus the decision maker maximizes the expected <u>discounted</u> present value of the <u>utility</u> of the payoff streams. Where X_t is the uncertain payoff to be received in time period t, $Eu(X_t)$ is its utility, and d^t is the discount applied to a "utility unit" received t periods in the future, the appropriate measure of well-being associated with the present prospect of receiving the gamble X_t after t periods is $d^t\, Eu(X_t)$. Similarly, the utility of an uncertain payment stream $(X_0, X_1, X_2, \ldots)$ is

$$(1)\quad U = Eu(X_0) + d\, Eu(X_1) + d^2\, Eu(X_2) + \ldots + d^t\, Eu(X_t) + \ldots$$

$$= \sum_t d^t\, Eu(X_t).$$ [3]

In the case of a continuous uncertain payment stream, X(t), we have

$$(2)\quad U = \int_0^\infty e^{-\rho t}\, Eu[X(t)]\, dt,$$

where ρ is a positive constant, the discount factor.

Therefore we need know only the decision maker's momentary utility function u(X) and his discount factor ρ in order to predict how we would evaluate any uncertain streams of payments. To do this, we simply transform all payments X into their utilities u(X), take expectations, and discount appropriately. (A convention that we shall adopt here is that monetary amounts are denoted by Greek letters and their utility equivalents are the corresponding Roman letters; i.e., $a = u(\alpha)$, $b = U(\beta)$.) If an activity has an initial cost of α and a benefit stream $\beta(t)$ $0 \leq t \leq m$, then the utility of that stream can be denoted

[3] See Hirschleifer, 1958; Arrow and Kurz, 1970; Koopmans, 1960.

$$(3) \quad u(-\alpha, \beta(t)) = -a + \int_{o}^{m} b(t) \qquad 0 \leq t \leq m$$

where $a = u(\alpha)$

$b(t) = u(\beta(t))$.

In earlier work on this problem, we assumed that the decision maker maximized the expected present monetary value (EMV) of the stream of payments, rather than the expected present utility of the stream of payments.[4] Such an assumption relieved us of the necessity of determining the subjective utility function for the individual, and allowed us to anticipate his decisions by observing objective data. Only under certain circumstances are the two maximands equivalent. There are two important situations in flood plains where that is the case.

First, if the individual can and does buy flood insurance at actuarially fair rates he has exchanged a random payoff with expectation m for a certain payoff of m. Then maximizing m is equivalent to maximizing $u(m)$, for $u(m)$ is certainly an increasing function of m. Thus, when flood insurance is available to the decision maker at fair rates, we can safely assume that he simply maximizes m.

The second case is where the amount of potential flood loss is small relative to the wealth of the decision maker. The utility function can be safely approximated by a straight line, because for a small enough range any continuous function can be approximated by a straight line. Now this is certainly not the case for the typical small landowner in a flood plain when he is considering his prospective flood losses. However, this is the case when the federal government is considering investments in flood plains. These investments are of such small magnitude compared to GNP that even if the nation were risk averse in the large, at this microscopic level it should be quite satisfactory to approximate the national "utility" function by a straight line. It should be noted that for the government this is the case without regard to whether the investment is public or private.[5]

---

[4]Brown, Contini, and McGuire, 1972; U.S. Army, 1967.

[5]See Baumol, 1968.

In summary, the simple expected present (monetary) value criterion is valid only if we are willing to assume that the stakes are very small, or the individual has flood insurance, or it is the government that is making the decision. When the random variable makes up a large part of someone's wealth we cannot use such a simple rule, but must instead take into account the decision maker's subjective utility function.

The Description of Available Activities

The landowner has available to him a variety of ways in which he can use his land. He can, for example, grow field crops, plant an orchard, build a gas station, a housing development, or a hotel. We shall assume that there are only a finite number of distinct opportunities, or activities, available. Each activity calls for some kind of capital equipment in concert with other inputs to produce an output or set of outputs. As long as a flood does not occur, the capital deteriorates in a known way. Capital deterioration will in general cause either a decrease in the amount of output or an increase in the amount of other inputs such as maintenance required to produce the same quantity of output. For completeness we shall consider "doing nothing" an activity; it is one of the feasible alternatives. The distinct economic activities available to the decision maker comprise his decision set.

We shall assume that prices are constant over time, and, in particular, are unaffected by floods. The initial cost of the capital equipment we denote by a, which is assumed to be positive. Since we know the quantity of output and the quantity of all inputs necessary to operate an activity of any age, we can calculate the flow of returns and the flow of costs resulting from operating an activity of any age. The difference between returns and costs of operating an activity of age τ will be called the <u>rate of net benefits</u> $b(\tau)$.[6] In general, $b(\tau)$ will decrease as capital deterioration proceeds. That need not always be the case, however. For

---

[6] These are the benefits as perceived in utility terms by the landowner. If he is not an EMV maximizer the actual cash flow will be $\beta(t)$ where $b(t) = \mu(\beta(t))$.

example, for an orchard which bore no fruit for several years b would be zero or negative for several years, would rise sharply, level off, and fall only many years later. For mathematical convenience we shall restrict ourselves to benefit streams which have only one peak: they may not oscillate.

Further, we shall abstract from technological change. If we were to try to analyze that complication, it would mean that both a and b would have still another time subscript, say τ_o, to indicate the date of the initial investment and hence the level of technology from which the activity is drawn. An activity in that more difficult case would be described by $[a(\tau_o), b(\tau, \tau_o)]$. Here we shall simply suppose that an activity can be completely described, for our purposes, by $[a, b(\cdot)]$, its initial cost and its stream of benefits over time. For the trivial case of doing nothing, $a = 0$ and $b(\tau) = 0$ for all τ.

When the discount rate is known there exists another way of describing an activity which is equivalent to $[a, b(\cdot)]$. It is the function $W(t)$ which is the present value in utility of the activity if it is started in the present and operated for t years without being interrupted by a flood. We define

$$(5) \quad W(t) = -a + \int_o^t b(\tau)\, e^{-\rho\tau}\, d\tau .$$

We shall assume that $b(\tau)$ is such that the integral exists; then $W(t)$ is finite for all t. By this we merely exclude from our discussion the economics of paradise. It should be noted that $W(t)$ the present value in utility is not the same as the utility of the discounted <u>monetary</u> value. That is, in general,

$$(6) \quad W(t) \neq u[-\alpha + \int_o^t \beta(\tau)\, e^{-\rho\tau}\, d\tau] .$$

The Choice of Replacement Date

Because capital deteriorates, there will usually come a time when it pays to discard the capital in place and start over again with brand new capital. It is up to the landowner to decide when that time is. Let m_i be the replacement age of capital of type i.

Then, m_i is a decision variable. In general it will be a function of the initial cost of equipment, the time profile of the benefit stream, the interest rate, and the intensity of the flood process (or equivalently, the frequency of floods). We shall analyze optimal replacement policy directly only in the third case that we consider. In the first two cases we shall proceed indirectly. There we shall achieve the optimization over possible replacement intervals as follows: Consider a number of arbitrarily fixed replacement intervals, that is, split the [a, b(·)] activity into [a, b(·), 1], [a, b(·), 2], [a, b(·), 3], ... etc., denoting replacement intervals (values of m_i) of 1, 2, 3, ... years. These shall be distinguished as "different activities." Then the choice of the optimal activity will simultaneously give us the approximately optimal value for m_i. Thus, in the first and second cases, activities will be formally described by [a, b(·), m], where m is an arbitrary fixed replacement policy, which is not necessarily optimal. In the third case, where the time for replacement is explicitly part of the problem, activities are sufficiently described by [a, b(·)].

The effect of replacement at m is to truncate $b(t)$ at m. This complicates the calculation of $W(t)$. If t is less than m, $W(t)$ is unchanged. If t is between m and $2m$, we have[7]

$$W^*(t) = W(m) + e^{-\rho m} W(t-m) \quad \text{if} \quad m < t < 2m$$

and similarly, if t is between jm and $(j+1)m$

$$(7) \quad W^*(t) = (1 + e^{-\rho m} + \dots + e^{-(j-1)\rho m}) W(m) + e^{-j\rho m} W(t-m) \quad \text{for} \quad jm < t < (j+1)m.$$

<u>The Effect of Floods</u>

Their effect, floods are understood to be instantaneous events and their effect on any of the activities is simply to remove or destroy the capital in place. The stream of payments generated by an

---

[7]We use $W^*(t)$ to denote present utility value for activities with fixed m.

activity is truncated by the flood and is identically zero as long as the activity is not replaced.[8]

The Probability of Floods

We shall assume that floods occur completely randomly over time. A mathematical model of such a random series of events is a Poisson process.[9] Think of floods happening over time. Let μ be the mean rate of occurrence, with dimension of the reciprocal of time. That is, if μ, the mean rate, is .5, the mean interval between floods is two years; if $u = .1$, the mean interval between floods is ten years; etc. Statisticians describe μ as the intensity of the process. Denote by $N_{t,t+h}$ the random variable which is the number of floods occurring in the interval of time $(t, t+h)$ where $h > 0$. Then the conditions for a flood process to be a Poisson process with intensity μ are that as $h \to 0$,

(8a) $\text{prob } (N_{t,t+h} = 0) = 1 - \mu h + o(h)$

(8b) $\text{prob } (N_{t,t+h} = 1) = \mu h + o(h)$

and that N is statistically independent of the number and position of events in the interval before t. These conditions imply that

(8c) $\text{prob } (N_{t,t+h} \geq 2) = o(h)$.

In the above, $o(h)$ denotes functions of h which tend to zero even faster than h, and hence can be disregarded in the limit. In a Poisson process these conditions hold for all t and for all h.

---

[8] The model can be expanded very easily to allow for floods which have effects either greater or less than completely destroying the activity in place. The procedure for handling this is exactly the same as that for handling relief payments to flood victims: payments (positive or negative) which are made every time that a flood occurs. See Chapter 6 below. Further adaptations of the model can be made for more complicated effects of floods, but the calculations are sufficiently complicated that they shall not be reproduced here. It suffices to say here that the effect of changing the severity of the flood, when that means reducing the cost of each flood without changing the probability distribution of floods, is exactly analogous to the effect of increasing flood relief payments, which is discussed in Chapter 6.

[9] This discussion is taken from Cox and Lewis, pp. 17-28.

To summarize, the main features of a Poisson process are that:

a. The probabilities in (8) do not change over time, so that there is no trend in the series;

b. the chance of two simultaneous events is negligible;

c. the probability of a flood in an interval starting at t is quite independent of what occurred before t.

These properties would seem to make the Poisson process the most appropriate mathematical model of a flood process. Indeed, another reason for choosing the Poisson process is that it or very closely related variants of it have been found in practice to give a good empirical fit to the occurrence of rate events like floods.[10]

The interval between events in a Poisson process is a random variable, T, which has a probability density function $\mu e^{-\mu T}$, and cumulative distribution function $F(T) = 1 - e^{-\mu T}$. This distribution is known as the <u>negative exponential distribution</u> (in some works it is called the <u>exponential distribution</u>). Its mean and variance are

$$E(T) = 1/\mu: \qquad Var\ (T) = 1/\mu^2.$$

Because the occurrences of events in any section of a Poisson process are independent of preceding sections of the process, T may also be interpreted as (a) the time from the origin to the first event, or (b) the time from any fixed time point until the next event, as well as (c) the interval between successive events. It

[10]The question of methods of statistical estimation of mean recurrence intervals for floods has been discussed at the highest level of government, the U.S. Water Resources Council. See U.S. Congress, Senate (1952) for a discussion of the various available methods and their similarities. Most of the methods, including the approved method, assume an underlying process which has the properties of the Poisson process. They are more complicated because they take into account seasonality and varying heights of floods. When seasonality is assumed away, as it is here, and only floods of a particular height or greater are considered, the resulting process is Poisson. Gumbel (1958) is the pioneer in this area of statistics; Van Dantzig (1956) considers a problem similar to ours, coastal flooding in the Netherlands. There he used a double exponential distribution to explain the frequency of various heights of floods. The best overall discussion of the problems of statistical inference about Poisson processes and related processes is in Cox and Lewis (1966).

should also be noted that successive intervals are mutually independent, each with probability density function $\mu e^{-\mu T}$.

The negative exponential distribution has a constant failure rate; failure rate is a term borrowed from renewal theory and is the conditional probability that an event will occur in the interval (t,t+dt). Denote it by $\mu(t)$ and

$$(9)\quad \mu(t) = f(t)/(1 - F(t))$$

$$= \frac{\mu e^{-\mu t}}{1 - (1 - e^{-\mu t})}$$

$$= \mu .$$

CHAPTER 3

THE CHOICE OF THE OPTIMAL ACTIVITY

Now let us characterize the choice of activity by the decision maker. In this chapter we shall assume that the decision maker knows that floods are generated by a Poisson process and that he knows what value μ takes. He thus knows all there is to know about the process exept when a flood will occur. A gambling analogue would be to enter a casino in Las Vegas where you knew the probability of winning in each of the available games, and you had to choose a game to play. This is in contrast to the next chapter where we assume that the landowner knows that floods are generated by a Poisson process but does not know what μ is.

The assumption made above that the flood process is a Poisson process is more restrictive than is required for the mathematical analysis here. It is sufficient for all the results in this chapter that flood intervals be independently and identically distributed. In terms of failure rates, our results would hold if failure rates were not constant over time as in the Poisson process but were a function of the time since the last flood.

We now turn to a very simple case in which to develop our model of investment choice. After we have developed the model and derived the results in the simple case we shall proceed to more complicated matters. Now, however, let us assume that after each flood the landowner shall contract for an investment program which he shall be required to follow until the next flood, whenever it comes. By investment program we mean that the landowner shall choose one of the activities in the set of available activities and he shall operate that activity until the next flood, renewing the capital each time the renewal age comes around. Only following the next flood will it be possible for him to <u>change</u> activities. Obviously this is an artificial problem, but it captures the basic structure of more complicated versions.

The states of the system are simply the dates of contracting, that is, the dates of floods (as well as zero, the starting date, when the initial contract is entered into). The set from which the states will beddrawn is simply the set of all nonnegative real numbers:

$$S = \{t: \ t \geq 0\}$$

There are n feasible activities which make up the set A of available acts. Each activity has associated with it the stream of payments it generates, described by $[a_i, b_i(\cdot), m_i]$ for i from 1 to n. Recall that a_i is the initial cost, $b_i(\cdot)$ is the stream of payments over time and m_i is the age at which the equipment should be replaced. The landowner must choose from the set one activity which he agrees to operate until the next flood. If the date of the flood is t; the state of the system is t_j. Then he chooses activity i from A. Then the system goes to state t_{j+1} where $t_{j+1} = t_j + T_j$, and $T_j > 0$ is the random interflood interval. For this transition he will receive a reward of $W_i^*(T_j)$ which has a present value to him of $e^{-\rho t_j} W_i^*(T_j)$. The reward generated by the transition from one state to the next is a function of the original state t_j, the act chosen i, and the new state $t_j + T_j$. It is

$$(1) \quad r(t_j, i, T_j) = e^{-\rho t_j} W_i^*(T_j), \qquad \begin{array}{l} i = 1, 2, \ldots, n \\ j = 1, 2, \ldots. \end{array}$$

When there is no ambiguity, we denote $r(t_j, i, T_j)$ by simply r.

The transition mechanism which moves the system from one state to the next is simply the flood process. Changes in state in the landowner's system are coincident with floods. The probability that any date will be the next state in the system is exactly the probability that the next flood will occur on that date. That probability is given to us by the probability density function for flood intervals, the negative exponential density function with intensity μ, which is $f(T) = \mu e^{-\mu T}$. The transition mechanism then is the probability statement,

(2) $$\text{prob}\ [t_{j+1} = t_j + T \mid t_j] = \begin{cases} \mu e^{-\mu T} & \text{if } T \geq 0 \\ 0 & \text{if } T < 0. \end{cases}$$

Since future states of the system are unknown, the landowner does not know the rewards for future changes of state, $r(t_j\ i, T_j)$, but knowing the transition mechanism he can calculate expectations. Since the landowner evaluates uncertain future rewards by their expected discounted utility, he has enough information to evaluate alternatives. For known value of μ we denote the expected reward of transition from state t_j to t_{j+1} with activity i in place as $E_\mu[r]$. From (10) we get

(3) $$E_\mu[r] = E_\mu[e^{-\rho t_j}\ W_i^*(T_j)].$$

Because the underlying stochastic process is Poisson, this expression is easy to evaluate. Since $t_j = \sum_{k=1}^{j-1} T_k$, and the T_j's are independently and identically distributed (i.i.d.) we have

(4) $$f(T_j) = \mu^{-\mu T_j}$$

and

(5) $$E_\mu[e^{-\rho t_j}\ W_i^*(T_j)] = (E_\mu\ e^{-\rho t_j})(E_\mu\ W_i^*(T)).$$

Concerning the first term in (14) we have

$$e^{-\rho t_j} = e^{(-\rho \sum_{k=1}^{j-1} T_k)}$$

If we take expectations,

$$E_\mu\ e^{-\rho t_j} = E_\mu\ e^{(-\rho \sum_{k=1}^{j-1} T_k)}$$

and, since the T_k's are i.i.d. as T,

$$(6) \qquad E_\mu\, e^{(-\rho \sum_{k=1}^{j-1} T_k)} = (E_\mu\, e^{-\rho T})^{(j-1)}$$

$$= [\int_o^\infty e^{-\rho T}\, \mu e^{\mu T}\, dT]^{(j-1)}$$

$$= (\frac{\mu}{\rho+\mu})^{(j-1)}.$$

Now we need $E_\mu\, W_i^*(T)$, the second term of (14):

$$(7) \qquad E_\mu\, W_i^*(T) = \int_o^\infty W_i^*(T)\, \mu e^{-\mu T}\, dT.$$

Thus we have

$$(8) \quad E_\mu[r] = (\frac{\mu}{\rho+\mu})^{(j-1)} [\int_o^\infty W_i^*(T)\, \mu e^{-\mu T}\, dT].$$

The states and the acts chosen at each state comprise a <u>history</u>, written as

$$(t_o, a_o, t_1, a_1, t_2, a_2, \ldots) \qquad t \in S,\ a \in A.$$

An <u>investment policy</u> is a sequence of decisions

$$\pi = (\pi_1, \pi_2, \pi_3, \ldots)$$

where each π_j is a function which chooses an element of the set of actions A based on the partial history to date.[1] Accordingly,

$$\pi_j = f(t_o, a_o, t_1, a_1, \ldots, t_{j-1}, a_{j-1}, t_j).$$

Notice that $\pi_o = f(t_o)$, so that all decisions depend on the initial state, t_o. Therefore, it is usual to write the whole policy as a function of the initial state, $\pi(t)$.

Every investment policy will generate a sequence of rewards as its history unfolds, and as we noted above, the landowner (in

[1]The decisions could include randomized policies, e.g., based on the flip of a coin. However, since Blackwell, 1965, shows that nothing is gained by randomizing a policy, we need not consider randomized policies.

principle) simply sums them to evaluate them, so if v is the evaluation at time zero of an entire history of rewards,

$$(9)\quad v(\pi) = \sum_{j=0}^{\infty} r(t_j, \pi_j, T_j)$$

$$= \sum_{j=0}^{\infty} e^{-\rho t_j} W^*_{\pi_j}(T_j).$$

But, of course, the future is unknown and $v(\pi)$ is also unknown, so we shall be concerned with the expected reward of any particular policy. We shall use capital V to denote the expectation of V, so

$$V(\pi,\mu) = E_\mu[v(\pi)]$$

$$(10)\quad = \sum_{j=0}^{\infty} E_\mu\,[r(t_j, \pi_j, T_j)]$$

$$= \sum_{j=0}^{\infty} E_\mu\,[e^{-\rho t_j} W^*_{\pi_j}(T)].$$

$V(\pi,\mu)$ is known as the expected value of policy π, with flood intensity μ.

In these terms, the investor's goal is to find the optimal investment policy, the policy which will give him the maximum value, i.e., maximum expected utility (maximum expected present monetary value if he is indifferent toward risk).

Denote the optimal policy $\tilde{\pi}$. Its value is given by the value function:

$$(11)\quad \tilde{V}(\mu) \equiv \max_{\pi} (V(\pi,\mu)).$$

In order for a maximization problem to be meaningful it must be shown that the function to be maximized is bounded from above. If not, we are talking about infinite returns and the economics of paradise. It is particularly simple to establish an upper bound on the value function here. The logic of the argument comes from the economics of the case. Since floods are destructive events, the best of all possible worlds in a flood plain is never to have a flood.[2] Equivalently, let μ, the intensity parameter of the distribution, be zero. Thus we have

$$V(\pi,\mu) \leq V(\tilde{\pi},0) \quad \text{for all } \pi.$$

If there are no floods, then all policies with the same initial activity are equivalent, since only the first decision is ever acted upon. Thus, there are only n distinct policies since there are only n elements in the set A. These policies are easy to evaluate:

$$V(\pi_i,0) = W_i^*(\infty), \qquad i = 1, \ldots, n$$

which exists by assumption. Thus,

$$(12) \quad \max_{i\varepsilon A} W_i^*(\infty) \geq V(\pi,\mu) \quad \text{for all } \pi \text{ and } \mu,$$

so that the value of the best unflooded activity is an upper bound for all policies for all values of μ.

Now we must find the landowner's optimal policy. To choose the best of all possible policies may seem at first to be too large an order, since the variety of possible policies is overwhelming, but we can use well-known results of dynamic programming to vastly simplify the task. This we are able to do because the underlying structure of the problem is very simple. Because the transition mechanism is a Poisson process, all that we can know about the future history of the flood process is contained in the intensity parameter. A knowledge of the past history of the process does not help us at all. Accordingly, the optimal policy will be found in the set of stationary policies, policies which depend only on the present state; they are independent of past history. We can restrict the set of likely candidates for an optimal policy even further. Knowing the

---

[2]One can think of instances when it is beneficial to have capital destroyed, but these are pathological cases where the pathology is induced by having chosen a value for m which is too high. We avoid these cases (because they are not appropriate in such an optimizing model) by assuming such activities, if they appear, are also accompanied by an activity with the same a and b(t) but with a better value for m.

present state of the system does not tell us very much; it only tells us the date of the latest investment commitment or contract. That information certainly does not tell us anything about the future or about what would be the best policy to follow. The optimal policy is really independent of the present state of the system; it depends only on μ, and μ does not change throughout the entire future of the system. Thus, if the optimal policy is stationary and independent of the present state, it must be a constant policy of the form "choose activity i always." The same point is made more apparent in the argument that follows.

Rewriting the value function for the optimal policy (11), we have

$$\tilde{V}(\mu) \equiv \max_{\pi} [V(\pi,\mu)].$$

Since the landowner's choice of investment has no effect on the timing of floods and since changes of state are caused only by floods, the future states of the system are independent of the policy followed.[3] That is, the dates t_1, t_2, ... are independent of the policy chosen by the landowner. Then, we can write out the value function for the optimal activity as follows:

$$(13)\quad \tilde{V}(\mu) = \max_i E_\mu W_i^*(T) + \max_i E_\mu W_i^*(T) \cdot E_\mu e^{-\rho t_1} + \max_i E_\mu W_i^*(T) \cdot E_\mu e^{-\rho t_2} + \ldots$$

From this it is clear that only one decision has to be made, and that is to find the optimal one-cycle activity.

Let $\tilde{i}$ be the activity which has the maximum expected reward over one flood cycle. Then the optimal policy is simply

$$\tilde{\pi} \equiv (\tilde{i}, \tilde{i}, \tilde{i}, \ldots).$$

---

[3]This assumption of investment having no effect on the timing of floods is restrictive. One can imagine situations where choice of investment does effect the probability of a flood. Lack of contour plowing or short-sighted timber-cutting practices or decreasing the capacity of the stream bed all increase the likelihood of floods.

If we define $\tilde{W}(\mu)$ as the expected value of the optimal activity over one flood cycle, then

$$(14)\quad \tilde{W}(\mu) = \max_i E_\mu W_i^*(T)$$

and from (6) and (13) we get

$$(15)\quad \tilde{V}(\mu) = \tilde{W}(\mu) \sum_{j=1}^{\infty} \left(\frac{\mu}{\rho+\mu}\right)^{(j-1)}$$

or

$$= \tilde{W}(\mu)\left(1 + \frac{\mu}{\rho}\right).$$

The value function can be restated in an interesting way, known as the principle of optimality, as follows:

$$(16)\quad \tilde{V}(\mu,t) = \max_i E_\mu W_i^*(T) + E_\mu e^{-\rho T} \cdot \tilde{V}(\mu,t+T).$$

This simply decomposes a sequential decision problem into the first decision and the remaining ones. The right-hand appearance of $\tilde{V}(\mu,t+T)$ denotes the value of operating the optimal policy, starting from a date T years later. Because of the simple structure of our problem $\tilde{V}(\mu)$ does not change with changes of state,

$$\tilde{V}(\mu,t) = \tilde{V}(\mu,t+T).$$

Explicit values for $V_i(\mu)$ have been derived for simple capital deterioration patterns. We present four examples: (1) the pattern of no decay, called the simple no-decay type, where the benefit rate is a constant b_i, (2) the one-hoss shay type, where the capital equipment continues as though new for m_i years whereupon it collapses to dust, (3) the exponential decay type, where benefits are assumed to decay exponentially at rate δ_i from the initial rate b_i, and (4) the delayed benefits type, which is essentially the simple no-decay type except that net benefits are zero until ℓ_i years after the capital is installed, at which point they jump to a constant rate of b_i. Figure 1 shows the time stream of benefits and costs for the four types of activity. More complicated capital deterioration patterns could be studied, but they complicate the analysis without clarifying the workings of the model.

Figure 1

simple no-decay

$b(t) = b$

one-hoss shay

$b(t) = \begin{cases} b & \text{for } t < m \\ 0 & t \geq m \end{cases}$

exponential decay

$b(t) = be^{-\delta t}$

delayed benefits

$b(t) = \begin{cases} b & \text{for } \ell \leq t \leq m \\ 0 & \text{otherwise} \end{cases}$

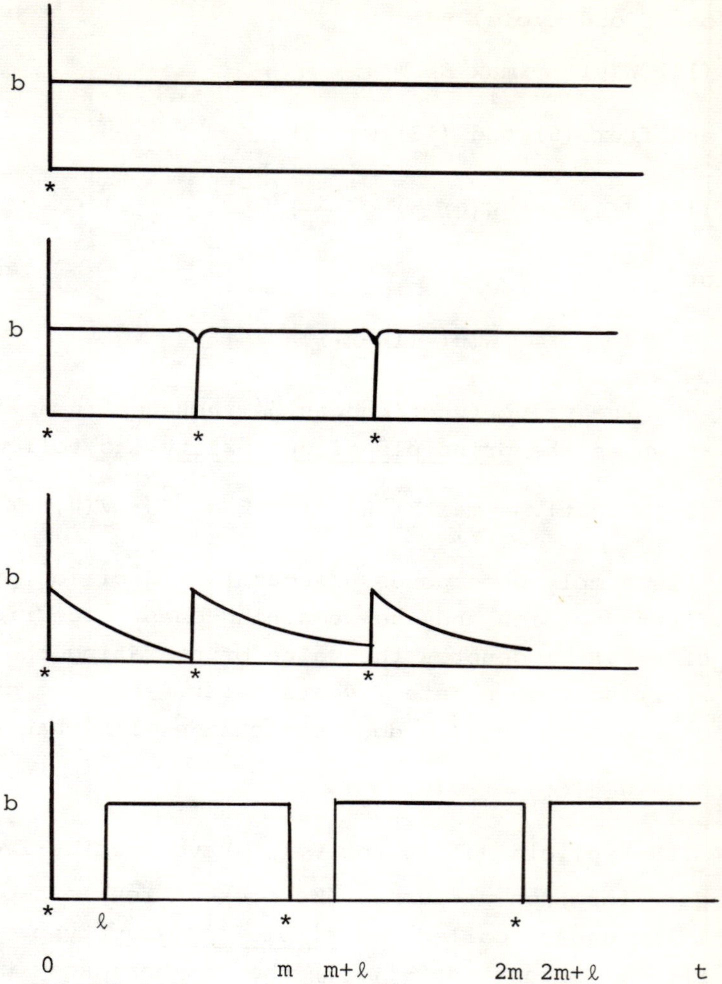

* marks time of rebuilding at cost a.

The value for these four types of activities can be derived after some algebraic manipulations. For a detailed discussion of the intermediate calculations see Brown, Contini, and McGuire (1972). The results, without calculations, are as follows:

No decay: $$V(\mu) = \frac{b}{\rho} - a(1 + \frac{\mu}{\rho})$$

One-hoss shay: $$V(\mu) = \frac{b}{\rho} - a(1 + \frac{\mu}{\rho}) \frac{1}{1 - e^{-(\mu+\rho)m}}$$

Exponential decay: $$V(\mu) = (1 + \frac{\mu}{\rho}) \left[-a + \frac{b(1 - e^{-(\mu+\rho+\delta)m})}{(\mu + \rho + \delta)} \right] \cdot \left[\frac{1}{1 - e^{-(\mu+\rho)m}} \right]$$

Delayed benefits: $$V(\mu) = \frac{b}{\rho} e^{-(\mu+\rho)} - a(1 + \frac{\mu}{\rho}).$$

CHAPTER 4

THE OPTIMAL REPLACEMENT POLICY

In the previous chapter we artificially restricted the choices available to the landowner in order to simplify our results. We allowed decisions only after floods.

Now we allow the landowner to change activities at any time he chooses. To do this we modify the structure of our problem slightly again and this time explicitly solve the optimal replacement interval problem. Instead of having m_i, the replacement interval, given to us in advance, we shall choose that interval as part of the problem. In general we expect the optimal interval will change with the flood intensity parameter. The more likely floods are, the less likely one is to earn sufficient returns to make early replacement worthwhile. This idea is perhaps more apparent in other situations: if the legal driving age is lowered to fifteen, I will postpone trading in my old car for a new one; in a war zone there is little replacement of buildings for any reason except war damage. Intuitively, the longer the replacement interval, the less often one exposes new capital to floods.

The state of the world is now described by three numbers instead of one. In addition to knowing the date, t, as before, we have to know the activity in place, i, and its age, τ. The date increases continuously, the i is unchanging until the landowner changes it or there is a flood, and τ increases with t until i changes. If the activity in place has been flooded, we shall call it activity 0. The state of the system is

$$s = (t, i, \tau) \qquad \text{where } t, \tau \geq 0$$
$$i \in \{0, 1, 2, \ldots, n\}.$$

The actions which are available to the decision maker in any state are to do nothing, or to replace the incumbent with any one of the n activities. Thus, the set of available actions, A, is augmented with one new alternative "make no changes," denoted 0.

The transition mechanism for this case is quite different in appearance from that in the earlier cases because we are adopting a different definition of the state of the system. Let us formulate the transition mechanism in terms of a small time interval from t to $t + dt$ where dt is small and positive. Call the state at time t, s, the action taken then, a, and the state at time $t + dt$, s'. Starting from a state (t, i, τ) four things can happen in the interval dt:

activity i is continued and

i. no flood occurs, or

ii. a flood does occur, or

activity i is replaced by activity j and

i. no flood occurs, or

ii. a flood does occur.

The new states and their probability given the action of the owner are, respectively:

	New State	Probability {State | Action}
(1.1)	$(t + dt, i, \tau + dt)$	$1 - \mu dt$
(1.2)	$(t + dt, 0, 0)$	μdt
(1.3)	$(t + dt, j, dt)$	$1 - \mu dt$
(1.4)	$(t + dt, 0, 0)$	μdt

When the incumbent activity i is left in place over the interval the reward of a transition is

$$e^{-\rho t} \int_o^{dt} b_i(\tau+x)\, e^{-\rho x}\, dx,$$

and since the interval is small the reward can be approximated by

(2.1,2) $\quad e^{-\rho t}\, b_i(\tau)\, dt.$

Also since the interval is small we can suppose that any flood that comes, comes at the end of the interval dt. Then the reward is independent of the occurrence of the flood. Using a similar argument for when a new activity j is put in place, the reward over dt is

(2.3,4) $\quad e^{-\rho t}[- a_j + \int_o^{dt} b_j(x)\, e^{-\rho x}\, dx] \tilde{=} e^{-\rho t}[-a_j + b_j(0)\, dt].$

To greatly simplify the exposition, let us assume for a moment that there is only one feasible activity, so $n = 1$. The problem then is to find the optimal replacement policy for that one activity.[1] This simplification allows us to write the value function V(s) in a more transparent way. Also, since there is only one activity we can drop all subscripts. When there is only one activity the possible states of the system are distinguished completely by the age of the equipment in place, τ. To avoid Greek letters let us replace τ with t in this section.

At any instant there are two acts available to the landowner: either he can do nothing or he can replace the equipment at a cost a. The value function accords with the principle of optimality of dynamic programming:

$$(3) \quad V(t) = \max \begin{cases} b(t)dt + e^{-\rho dt}[(1-\mu dt)V(t+dt) + \mu dt\, V(0)], \\ -a + b(0)dt + e^{-\rho dt}[(1-\mu dt)\, V(dt) + \mu dt\, V(0)]. \end{cases}$$

The first line gives the expected present value (at time t) of deciding to do nothing; the second line gives the expected present value of deciding to replace. The impact of a flood is found entirely within the brackets. The last term in each line shows the expected value of having to start all over again because of the flood.

Because renewal requires an immediate payment of $-a$, $\lim_{dt \to 0} V(dt) = V(0) + a$. As dt approaches zero, the principle of optimality becomes

$$(4) \quad V(t) = \max\,[V(t),\, V(0)].$$

Thus as long as $V(t) > V(0)$, the landowner will do nothing. As soon as $V(t)$ declines to $V(0)$, that is, $V(t) = V(0)$, he will choose to replace. The value taken by t when $V(t) = V(0)$ will be the <u>optimal replacement interval</u>. In keeping with our earlier notation, we shall call the optimal replacement interval m_i for activity i $(i = 1, 2, \ldots, n)$.

Assume that the best alternative is to do nothing; so the first alternative is the maximizing one. Then

$$(5) \quad V(t) = b(t)dt + e^{-\rho dt}[(1-\mu dt)\, V(t+dt) + \mu dt\, V(0)].$$

---

[1]The method of analysis used here is adapted from Beckmann, 1968, section 27.

We shall use the Taylor's expansion of $e^{-\rho dt}$ and $V(t+dt)$ in what follows ($o(dt)$ denotes terms of higher order than dt):

$$(6) \quad e^{-\rho dt} = 1 - \rho dt + o(dt),$$

and

$$(7) \quad V(t+dt) = V(t) + dt\, V'(t) + o(dt) \quad \text{for} \quad t > 0.$$ [2]

Substituting (6) and (7) into (5) we get

$$(8) \quad V(t) = b(t)dt + [1 - \rho dt + o(dt)]\{(1 - \mu dt) [V(t) + dt\, V'(t) + o(dt)] + \mu dt\, V(0)\}.$$

Cancelling $V(t)$, dividing through by dt and letting dt go to zero, we get the differential equation

$$(9) \quad V'(t) - (\rho + \mu)\, V(t) = - b(t) - \mu\, V(0).$$

Multiplying by $e^{-(\rho+\mu)t}$, we get

$$(10) \quad (V(t)\, e^{-(\rho+\mu)t})' = - b(t)\, e^{-(\rho+\mu)t} - \mu\, V(0)\, e^{-(\rho+\mu)t}.$$

Integrating, it follows that

$$(11) \quad V(t)\, e^{-(\rho+\mu)t} = C - \int_0^t b(x)\, e^{-(\rho+\mu)x}\, dx - V(0) \frac{\mu}{\rho + \mu} (1 - e^{-(\rho+\mu)t}),$$

or

$$(12) \quad V(t) = C\, e^{(\rho+\mu)t} - e^{(\rho+\mu)t} \int_0^t b(x)\, e^{-(\rho+\mu)x}\, dx + V(0) \frac{\mu}{\rho + \mu} (1 - e^{(\rho+\mu)t})$$

where C is the **constant** of integration, which we evaluate by letting t go to zero. Because of the discontinuity at $V(0)$ we have $\lim_{t \to 0} V(t) = V(0) + a$, so

$$(13) \quad V(0) + a = C.$$

---

[2]Prime denotes time derivative.

Rewriting (12), we get

$$(14)\quad V(t) = ae^{(\rho+\mu)t} - e^{(\rho+\mu)t}\int_0^t b(x)\, e^{-(\rho+\mu)x}\,dx + V(0)\left[\frac{\mu + \rho\, e^{-(\rho+\mu)t}}{\rho + \mu}\right].$$

The condition for replacement to be optimal at time m is that $V(m) = V(0)$ by the principle of optimality. Or, using (14)

$$(15)\quad V(0) = V(m) = ae^{(\rho+\mu)m} - e^{(\rho+\mu)m}\int_0^m b(x)\, e^{-(\rho+\mu)x}\,dx + V(0)\left[\frac{\mu + \rho\, e^{-(\rho+\mu)m}}{\rho + \mu}\right].$$

Now multiply by $e^{-(\rho+\mu)m}$ and re-arrange to get

$$(16)\quad V(0) = \left[-a + \int_0^m b(x)\, e^{-(\rho+\mu)x}\,dx\right]\left[\frac{\rho + \mu}{\rho(1 - e^{-(\rho+\mu)m})}\right].$$

From (16) it is obvious that $V(0)$ depends on m, the replacement interval. To remind us of that we shall write $V(0)$ as $V(0,m)$.

Using (16) we can now rewrite (14) explicitly as

$$(17)\quad V(t,m) = ae^{(\rho+\mu)t} - e^{(\rho+\mu)t}\int_0^t b(x)\, e^{-(\rho+\mu)x}\,dx + \left[-a + \int_0^m b(x)\, e^{-(\rho+\mu)x}\,dx\right]\left[\frac{\mu + \rho\, e^{(\rho+\mu)t}}{\rho(1 - e^{-(\rho+\mu)m})}\right].$$

The next step is to find the optimizing m. This we can do by setting the derivative of $V(0,m)$ with respect to m equal to zero. This is equivalent to $\frac{dV(t,m)}{dm} = 0$ since $\frac{dV(t,m)}{dV(0,m)}$ is a positive constant.

To simplify the calculation of the derivative of $V(0,m)$ let us rewrite (16) as

$$V(0,m) = A \cdot B$$

where

$$A = -a + \int_0^m b(x)\, e^{-(\rho+\mu)x}\,dx$$

and

$$B = \frac{\rho + \mu}{\rho(1 - e^{-(\rho+\mu)m})}.$$

We have

$$\frac{dA}{dm} = b(m)\ e^{-(\rho+\mu)m}$$

and

$$\frac{dB}{dm} = - B^2\ \rho\ e^{-(\rho+\mu)m}.$$

Now we can easily evaluate the derivative and set it equal to zero:

$$(18)\quad \frac{dV(0,m)}{dm} = - A\ B^2\ \rho\ e^{-(\rho+\mu)m} + B\ b(m)\ e^{-(\rho+\mu)m}$$
$$= B\ e^{-(\rho+\mu)m}\ (b(m) - \rho\ V(0,m)) = 0.$$

Since $B\ e^{-(\rho+\mu)m}$ is positive we can ignore it, and we get

$$(19)\quad b(\tilde{m}) = \rho\ V(0,\tilde{m}).$$

The tilde indicates the optimal value of m.

This has an economic interpretation. For a maximal return per unit of time, it is necessary that the average return over time $[\rho\ V(0,\tilde{m})]$ be equal to the marginal return from postponing renewal an infinitesimal amount of time $[b(\tilde{m})]$. The optimal value for m can be found by solving (18) using standard numerical techniques. When the benefit stream exhibits exponential decay ($b(t) = be^{-\delta t}$), the conditions for optimal m have been found (see U.S. Army, 1967, pp. 110-112).

Now that we have discussed the problem of optimal replacement when there is only one activity available, let us return to the more general problem where there are n activities from which to choose. Without loss of generality, let Activity 1 be in place for τ years without a flood. Then the state of the system is $(t, 1, \tau)$. How do we find our optimal replacement policy from here? First, we know that the optimal policy eventually will be stationary, so we can divide the problem into two parts: when to replace the incumbent Activity 1, and what to do thereafter. We need to know the second part in order to solve the first. Therefore, assume that the incumbent has been removed and we have to determine our optimal stationary policy, which is equivalent to finding the optimal activity and its optimal replacement interval. First, we calculate the optimal replacement interval $\tilde{m}_i$ and the value function $V_i(0,\tilde{m}_i)$ for each of the n activities. Choose the maximum of these n values and call it $\tilde{V}(0)$ and call the corresponding activity $\tilde{i}$.

Now we can return to the first part of the problem, which is to find when to replace the incumbent activity. The optimality principle holds here:

$$V(t, 1, \tau) = \max [V(t, 1, \tau), V(t, \tilde{i}, 0)].$$

The incumbent activity should be replaced as soon as

$$V(t, 1, \tau) = V(t, \tau, 0)$$

or at the next flood, whichever happens first.

CHAPTER 5

WHEN FLOOD PROBABILITIES ARE UNKNOWN: THE BAYESIAN APPROACH

Introduction

When the flood intensity parameter μ is not known with certainty, we cannot directly apply the results derived in the previous two chapters because they depend on the value of μ. In this chapter, therefore, we need to develop an adaptive policy, which takes best advantage of whatever knowledge about the flood process is available. In fact, it is usually the case that we do not know the value of μ with certainty. Floods are often such infrequent events that it takes a long time to develop a statistically reliable estimate of the probability of larger floods. For most areas of the United States accurate records of floods have been kept for less than a hundred years. This is a very short sample to use to predict a flood of the size which comes every fifty or hundred years on the average. Generally, we do not know the probability distribution of the inter-flood intervals of major floods. Hydrologists, however, are willing to make assumptions about the form of this probability distribution. Using the assumed form of the distribution they estimate values for the parameters of the distribution, based on the available statistical evidence. For the reasons discussed in Chapter 1 we shall continue to assume that the flood process behaves as if it were a Poisson process. Then it is necessary to estimate only one parameter--μ.

Here we shall consider an investment policy which takes into account the uncertainty the owner has about the true value of μ. We shall see how his policy adapts to the new information he gains by observing the flood process over time. First, we shall have to develop a description of his state of knowledge at any time, and then we shall turn to the effect of changes in the state of his knowledge on his investment policy. In contrast to Chapters 3 and 4 where results are available for all the cases, the computational complexity here overwhelms efforts to get results in the more general cases; we can only indicate the structure of the problems involved and indicate our conjectures about optimal investment policies.

Incomplete Information About μ

Consider the problem facing a man who owns a piece of land in a flood plain when he does not have perfect information about the true value of μ the intensity parameter of floods that affect his land. Nevertheless, he has to decide what activity to operate on the land right now and take responsibility for it. What should he do? Obviously he should make the best use of information available to him and hope that he is right. But this is vague counsel. Should he guess at μ and then apply the theory of Chapters 3 and 4? Should he work out the recommendations of Chapters 3 and 4 for several different values of μ and then average the results--whatever that might mean? Or must he disregard the methods of Chapters 3 and 4 entirely? Our purpose here is to make precise what it means to "make the best use of information available."

Our approach here is what is called the Bayesian view. We shall presume that the landowner's degree of belief can be described by a probability distribution. As the landowner learns more about the underlying phenomenon, he adjusts his beliefs in a consistent fashion. At any given date his subjective uncertainty is indistinguishable from any "objective" uncertainty that might also be in his decision problem. He is assumed to take that decision which maximizes his expected utility.

Let us first assume that he is willing to act as if floods were controlled by a process the form of which is Poisson with unknown parameter μ. He believes that flood intervals occur as if they were generated by a stochastic process as independent random variables $T_1, T_2, T_3, \ldots$ with identical densities of the negative exponential form $f(T) = \mu e^{-\mu T}$. Independence implies first of all that floods are not controlled by a benevolent or malevolent being doling out rewards or punishment for actions taken by the mortals in the flood plain: floods do not come because the farmer's crops are ready for harvest, etc. It also rules out seasonality or wet and dry "spells" that are anything other than random. Incidentally, seasonality can be handled rather easily.[1] "Spells" make the probability

[1]See Cox and Lewis, 1966, p. 28.

calculations considerably more complicated, but still possible. μ is no longer constant but becomes time dependent $(\mu(t))$.

The Description of Beliefs and of Learning

Once we agree that the flood process is a Poisson process, our next step is to find a mathematical way of describing the landowner's beliefs about the parameter μ, or equivalently about $1/\mu$, the mean flood interval. The obvious way of formulating his beliefs about μ is as a probability distribution over the true value of μ. Here probability is to be construed as a measure of the degree of his belief, not as the relative frequency of μ taking a certain value. A relative frequency interpretation would be absurd, since the true value of μ is fixed.

If beliefs are described by a probability distribution, then learning means changing that probability distribution to take account of what has been learned. Consequently, it would make our analysis considerably simpler if we could confine our attention to a family of distributions such that each member is easily described and learning simply moves us from one member of the family to another. If the individual's beliefs are very complete and exact, of course, they might not fit into a distribution which is a member of such a convenient family, and we could not just proceed so nicely from one member to the next. But usually one's beliefs are not so exact; one might have feelings about the mean or range or median and maybe even the variance, but probably not much more. In this case, the analyst has more freedom and can use a distribution which is a member of a convenient family and is consistent with the individual's vague beliefs. Given that the landowner's beliefs are sufficiently vague that they can be adequately described by a member of a simply characterized family, then we should choose a family which is convenient and easily interpreted.

The best candidate for that family in our problem is the family of "gamma-1" distributions.[2] The gamma-1 distribution is a two-parameter distribution. Each pair of values for the parameters defines a new distribution for μ. Conveniently, the two parameters,

---

[2]See Raiffa and Schlaifer, 1961, p. 227.

call them r and t, have very simple interpretations. The probability density function for the true value of μ, called here $\gamma(\mu|r, t)$, can be interpreted as the density one would derive from observing the process t years and seeing r floods.

$$(1) \quad \gamma(\mu|r,t) = \frac{e^{-\mu t} \, (\mu t)^{r-1}}{(r-1)!} \, t. \qquad \mu \geq 0$$
$$r,t = 1, 2, 3, \ldots$$

The expected value of μ is

$$(2) \quad \bar{\mu} = \frac{r}{t}$$

and the variance is

$$(3) \quad \text{var}\,(\mu) = \frac{r}{t^2}.$$

The convenience of the gamma-1 distribution derives from the fact that when the prior distribution is gamma-1 with parameter (r', t') and an additional sample observation of the process yields (r,t), it can be shown that the posterior distribution will be gamma-1 with parameters (r", t") where

$$r'' = r' + r \qquad t'' = t' + t.$$[3]

Accordingly it is very simple to take into account new information about the flood process, that is, what the landowner learns from experience.

Our landowner starts working his land in the year zero, when his beliefs about the flood process can be described by a distribution with density $\gamma(\mu|r_o, t_o)$: that is, his initial "prior" distribution is that gamma-1 distribution with parameters (r_o, t_o).[4] After, say, ten years of observation, in which he has seen perhaps two floods, his current priors would be $(r_o + 2, t_o + 10)$. In general, at date X, up to which time he has observed n_x floods, his priors would be $(r_o + n_x, t_o + X)$. Clearly, the state of his

---

[3] Raiffa and Schlaifer, 1961, p. 227.

[4] We use "prior" here in the same way as Raiffa and Schlaifer, that is, as a synonym for beliefs.

beliefs is a stochastic process, depending on his initial prior distribution and on his observations of the flood process. Observations of the flood process are equivalent to samples drawn from the process.

This is a good place to record some of the properties of statistical distributions related to the gamma-1 for which we shall have use later. The "inverted beta-2" distribution for a random variable S has the density

$$(4) \quad g(S|n,r,t) = \frac{(n+r-1)!\, S^{n-1}\, t^{r}}{(n-1)!\,(r-1)!\,(t+S)^{n+r}} \qquad t,S \geq 0 \quad n,r = 1, 2, 3, \ldots$$

It can easily be shown that if floods occur according to the $\gamma(\mu|r,t)$ process then the distribution of T, the inter-flood interval, in terms of r and t, is

$$(5) \quad \int_0^\infty f(T|\mu)\, \gamma(\mu|r,t)\, d\mu = g(T|1,r,t) = r \frac{t^r}{(t+T)^{r+1}},$$

and the expected interval is

$$(6) \quad E(T|r,t) = \frac{t}{r-1}.$$ [5]

Similarly, the density of the sum of the next n flood cycles, $S_n = T_1 + T_2 + \ldots + T_n$, for given prior distribution (r,t), is

$$(7) \quad g(S_n|n,r,t),$$

the inverted beta-2. The density of the $(n+1)^{th}$ flood cycle conditional on the first n is

$$g(T_{n+1}|1, r+n, t+S_n).$$

So we see that the prior distribution of intervals is always in the inverted beta-2 family, just as the prior distribution of μ is always in the gamma-1 family.

---

[5] Since for the inverted beta-2 distribution, $E(S|n,r,t) = \frac{n}{r-1} t$. See Raiffa and Schlaifer, 1961, p. 279.

It is instructive to consider the situation graphically. The development of prior-distribution parameters appears as a step function in r and t. Figure 2 gives a sample history.

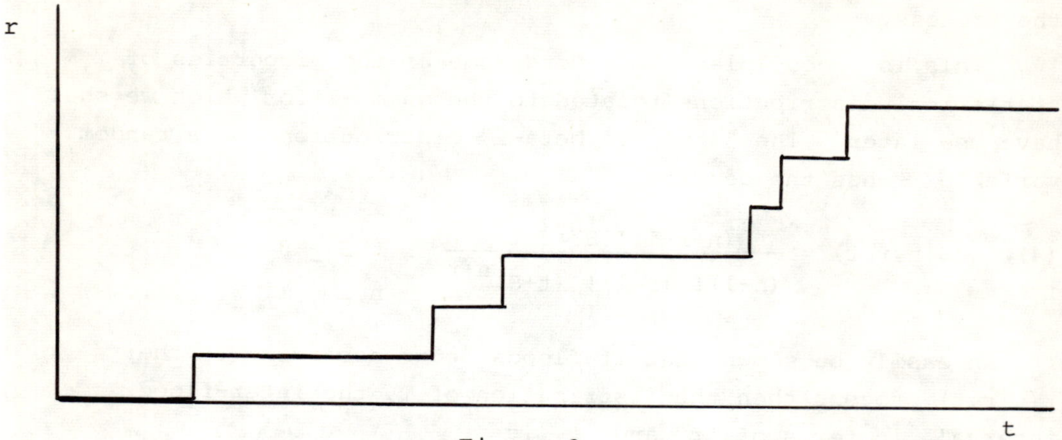

Figure 2

Sample History of Beliefs About a Flood Process

There is a continuous increase in t while r increases by one every time there is a flood. The probability of attaining any feasible (r,t) combination from any other (r,t) combination is known and can be derived from expression (7). Notice that the slope of a line from the origin to any point on the plane gives the expected value of μ, (r/t).

The Simple Case: Investment Contracts can only be Made After Floods

Now we shall turn our attention to developing an adaptive dynamic program. It is necessary to include in the description of state of the system information about the state of the landowner's beliefs and to take them into account in the transition mechanism as well.

When μ was known the state of the system was completely described by the date of the flood and the transitions were from flood date to flood date. Now we must also take account of the changes in beliefs about floods that take place as the system proceeds from flood to flood. If we know the initial values of the priors (r_o, t_o), then the system is completely described by the new values for r and t at each state because the date, which is sufficient for the physical system, is simply $t - t_o$. The set of states is then

$$S = \{r,t: \; r = r_o + 1, \; r_o + 2, \; \ldots; \; t \geq t_o\}.$$

That is, the r's are integers greater than the initial r_o and the t's are real numbers greater than t_o. As before, at every state (r,t) the landowner must choose an activity which he will operate until the next flood.

The set of activities from which he must choose is, of course, unchanged. Similarly, the payoff structure is identical to the case when flood probabilities are known. Thus if Activity i is chosen at date t and operated for T years, the payoff will be $W_i^*(T)\, e^{-\rho t}$.

The transition mechanism is changed from that in previous chapters because the "system" now includes the beliefs of the landowner about floods. Each transition of the system does two things; it brings him a reward and it gives him more information about the unknown parameter μ. Previously the distribution of T was conditional on knowing the true value of μ. Now we must use the unconditional distribution, based only on our prior beliefs. The transition mechanism is

$$\text{(8)} \quad \text{prob}\,(r+1,\; t+T \,|\, r,t) = g(T\,|\,1,r,t) \quad \text{for} \quad T \geq 0$$

$$= \frac{r\,t^r}{(t+T)^{r+1}}\,.$$

No other transitions are possible.

The reward structure is unchanged from the earlier problem, but the notation is slightly different:

$$\text{(9)} \quad r[(r,t),\; i,\; (r+1,\; 1+T)] = e^{-\rho(t-t_o)}\, W_i^*(T). \quad i = 1, 2, \ldots, n.$$

The expectation of $W_i^*(T)$ conditional on (r,t) we shall denote $E_{r,t}\, W_i^*$.

$$\text{(10)} \quad E_{r,t}\, W_i^* = \int_o^\infty W_i^*(T)\; g(T\,|\,1,\, r,t)\; dT.$$

The expected reward of the nth transition after state (r,t), conditional on its starting date $(t - t_o + S_n)$ where $S_n = T_1 + T_2 + \dots + T_n$, is

$$(11)\quad E_{r,t+S_n} W_i^*(T_{n+1}) = e^{-\rho(t-t_o+S_n)} E_{r+n,t+S_n} W_i^*.$$

The unconditional expected reward can be calculated

$$(12)\quad E_{r,t} W_i^*(T_{n+1}) = e^{-\rho(t-t_o)} \int_o^\infty e^{-\rho S_n} E_{r+n,t+S_n} W_i^* g(S_n|n,r,t)\, dS_n.$$

To be sure the problem is well defined we must show that a maximum exists, i.e., that it is bounded from above. The argument is identical to that in the last chapter. The value of any policy is not greater than the value of the optimal policy when the true μ is known which in turn is no greater than $V(0)$. Therefore, the problem is well defined.

An adaptive policy or investment program is a policy which specifies an activity in A (or perhaps a distribution on the set A) depending on the history of the system to date. A stationary policy chooses an act in A based only on the current state. In other words, a stationary policy can be conceived of as a partition of S, the set of states, into subsets S_j so that when the system is in a state in S_j the policy will choose activity j (some of the subsets may be empty). The value of any policy $\pi = (\pi_o, \pi_1, \pi_2, \dots)$ is its expected utility,

$$(13)\quad V_\pi(r,t) = \sum_{j=0}^{\infty} E_{r,t} W^*_{\pi_j} (T_{j+1}).$$

Again, the optimal policy $\tilde{\pi}$ has the value

$$(14)\quad V(r,t) = \max_\pi [V_\pi(r,t)].$$

It is instructive to write the value of the optimal program in accord with the optimality principle:

$$(15)\quad V(r,t) = \max_i E_{r,t} W_i^*(T) + E_{r+1,t+T}\, e^{-\rho T} V(r+1, 1+T).$$

Since T is unaffected by the choice of activity, the second term is independent of our choice and we can decompose the problem into a series of choices, one each cycle. This is the clue to the optimal policy. The optimal policy is to choose, at each state, that activity which has the maximum $E_{r,t} W_i^*$. Bhattacharjee has proven that indeed this is the optimal policy (Bhattarcharjee, 1968). The optimal program then is straightforward to describe: choose the activity with the highest expected one-cycle return. Unfortunately, the complicated nature of the transition probabilities makes the calculation of V(r,t) very difficult. So far, efforts to represent the value of such policies in closed form have not met with success. However, it is possible to derive upper and lower bounds for the value of the optimal policy.[6]

Consider a landowner who has two activities available. In Figure 3 we graph the value of operating the activity forever as a function of μ, the true flood parameter. Let $\tilde{V}(\mu)$ be the maximum for each μ, the value of the optimal policy if μ is known (as derived in Chapter 1). In Figure 4 we graph the probability density function of μ based on the landowner's present beliefs (r,t).

Bhattacharjee (1968), (Theorem 6.1) shows that the expected value of the static policy, "always choose Activity i, whatever you learn in the meantime," denoted $V_i(r,t)$, is

$$(16)\quad V_i(r,t) = \int_o^\infty V_i(\mu)\ \gamma(\mu|r,t)\ d\mu.$$

The optimal policy V(r,t) must be at least as good as the best static policy; in particular,

$$(17)\quad V(r,t) \geq \max_i V_i(r,t).$$

This gives us a lower bound to the optimal policy. The difference between the two sides of (17) is the expected return due to future learning.

---

[6]See Bhattacharjee (1968).

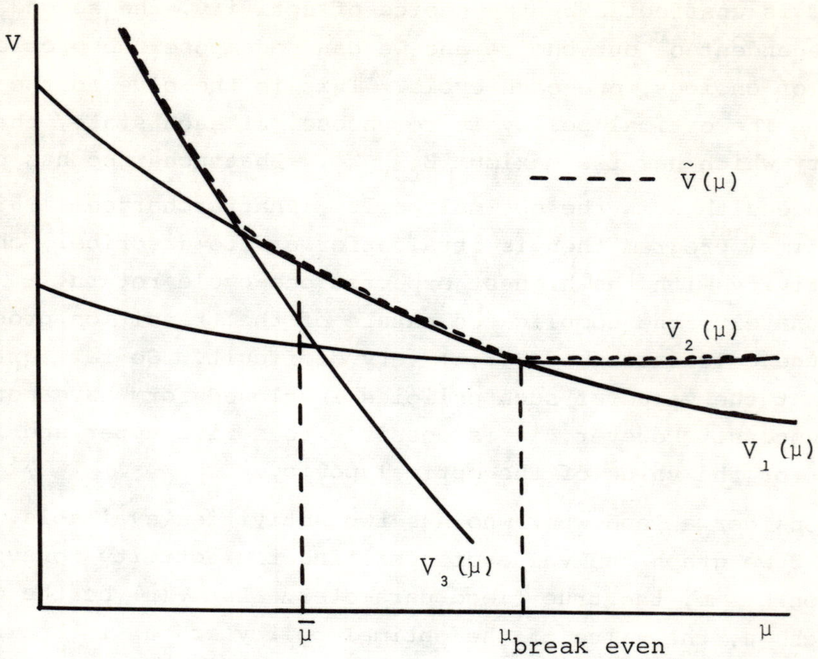

Figure 3

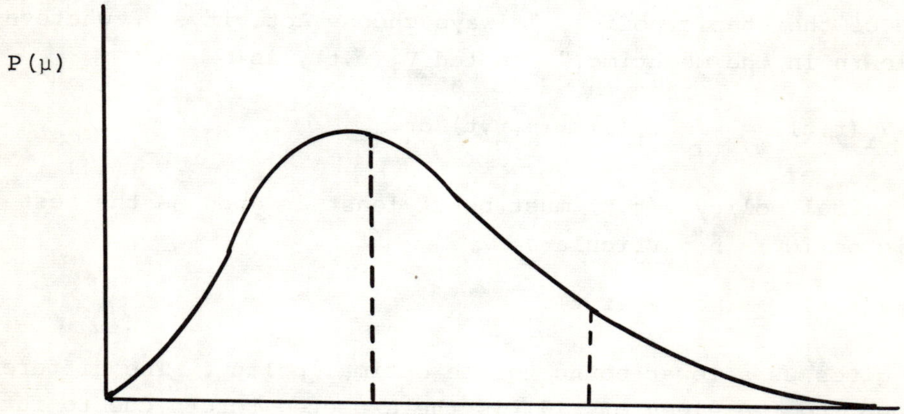

Figure 4

It is also shown there that an upper bound to $V(r,t)$ is

$$(18)\quad \int_0^\infty \tilde{V}(\mu)\ \gamma(\mu|r,t)\ d\mu.$$

To interpret this, consider Figures 3 and 4. Expression (18) is the value of the optimal program $\tilde{V}(\mu)$ for known μ, weighted by beliefs about μ. In other words, this is the expected return to finding out the true μ immediately. That return cannot be less than the best policy based on any slow learning process.

The difference between the value of the optimal policy and the expected value of $\tilde{V}(\mu)$ given (r,t) is known as the expected value of perfect information, EVPI (r,t):

$$(19)\quad \text{EVPI}\ (r,t) \equiv \int_0^\infty \tilde{V}(\mu)\ \gamma(\mu|r,t)\ d\mu - V(r,t).$$ [7]

The more information is gained about the process, the more concentrated the distribution is about the true μ and the less weight is given to any mistakes in the tails. It becomes more likely that the activity chosen is correct, and less likely that there will be a loss.

When the process has been observed for a long time, there is little to be gained from observing it more, even little to be gained from knowing μ absolutely without error. The bounds converge.

An Intermediate Case

When renewal of the system is allowed both immediately after floods and when equipment is of age m (where m is specified beforehand), the problem of finding the optimal policy is considerably more complicated--so much so, in fact, that we have not been able to find it. However, there are some interesting things which can be said about it.

The set of possible states is unchanged from the last case, as are the set of feasible activities and the reward structure. What

---

[7] See Raiffa, 1968, p. 27.

changes from the last case and what gives us so much trouble is the transition mechanism. The transition probabilities are now a function of the choice of activity because it is impossible for the next transition to come later than m_i years from now. The next state is a function of the present state <u>and</u> the choice made now (because of the m_i associated with it). If s and $s' \in S$ are consecutive states and $i \in A$ is the activity chosen at state s, and $q(\cdot|\cdot)$ denotes a conditional probability density function, the transition mechanism from s to s' is

$$(20)\quad q(s'|s,i) = \begin{cases} q(r+1,\ t+T|r,t,i) = g(T|1,r,t) \\ \text{if there is a flood at } T \text{ for } 0 \leq T < m_i \\ q(r,t+m_i|r,t,i) = 1 - G(m_i|1,r,t) \\ \text{otherwise,} \end{cases}$$

where $g(\cdot|\cdot)$ is the inverted beta-2 density function and $G(\cdot|\cdot)$ is the corresponding cumulative distribution function.

The optimal policy, whatever it is, must conform to the optimality principle: For all $i \in A$,

$$(21)\quad V(s) = \max_i E_s W_i^* + E_s e^{-\rho T} V(s');$$

where

$$(22)\quad E_s W_i^* = \int_0^{m_i} W_i^*(T)\, g(T|1,r,t)\, dT + [e^{-\rho m_i} W_i(m_i)] [1 - G(m_i|1,r,t)]$$

and

$$(23)\quad E_s e^{-\rho T} V(s') = \int_0^{m_i} e^{-\rho T} V(r+1,\ t+T)\, g(T|1,r,t)\, dT + [1 - G(m_i|1,r,t)]\, [e^{-\rho m_i} V(r,t+m_i)].$$

Equation (21) should be compared with equation (15), the optimality equation for the last case. In (21) we cannot separate the first and subsequent decisions as we could in (15) because the distribution of the discount factor $e^{-\rho T}$ in the second term is a function of the initial decision.

The difference between the first and second cases is that in the second case the landowner has more opportunities to change his mind. He will avail himself of these opportunities only if he feels that earlier decisions were wrong. This feeling is a result of information gained since the last decision. When t is relatively large, that is, when the process has been observed for a long time, one would expect relatively little information to be gained between renewals. This is a situation when the optimal policy would be very similar to that in the first case, namely, choose that activity which has the highest expected one-cycle return, assuming it is rebuilt every renewal until the flood. Another situation where the optimal policy is similar would be when the discount rate is high and the replacement interval is long. When the replacement interval is long the freedom to change one's mind at that time is not worth very much, especially if the interest rate is high.

Certainly the value of the optimal policy here is at least as high as the value of the optimal policy in the first case. That is true by the definition of optimality, because every policy which is available in the first case is available in the second, in addition to others. The value of the optimal policy here is bounded from above by expression (18) for the same reasons as in the first case.

The chapter on computer simulation describes a computer program designed to simulate a history of a landowner who can change activities at the end of a given replacement interval as well as after a flood. The decision rule simulated there is that he chooses that activity which has the highest $V(\overline{\mu})$, where $\overline{\mu} = r/t$, his current estimate of the value of μ. That is, he acts as if his estimate of μ were in fact true and chooses a policy accordingly.

The Case Where Replacement is Possible at any Time

When replacement is possible at any time, there are no concrete results available in the adaptive programming framework. We can only make the same kind of general statements as we made about the previous case. As information increases, the optimal policy will come to look more and more like the optimal static policy when the true value of μ is known. Also, since every policy available in the previous case is available in this case, the value of the optimal policy here must be at least as great as the value of the optimal policy there. The value of the optimal policy is bounded from above by expression (18), for the same reasons as in the two previous cases. It should be pointed out that the main difference between the second and third cases derives from the fact that the optimal replacement period depends on the value of μ, hence on r and t. Now the optimal m_i, we would expect, is not very elastic with respect to the value of μ. Therefore, once we have even a gross estimate of the value of μ, we should be very close to the optimal replacement age for the activity. If that is the case, the optimal policy in the replacement case is very similar to the optimal policy in the second case. Thus, we would not be far wrong if we used the present estimate of the optimal m_i as a proxy for the future optimal values of m_i which puts us back into the intermediate case.

CHAPTER 6

FLOOD CONTROL AND RELIEF MEASURES: AN ELEMENTARY VIEW

Now that we have developed a theory of individual investment behavior in a flood plain, we shall use it to analyze how individuals in the flood plain can be expected to respond to government policy measures. The kinds of policy that we shall consider here are physical flood protection works such as dams, levees, and the like, flood insurance, disaster relief programs, and flood plain zoning. The purpose of the analysis here is to show how the model of individual behavior developed above throws light on the policy problems faced by government. It is not intended to be a full scale analysis of any particular policy. Any practitioner should recognize the great simplification involved in our analysis, but hopefully he would find here the elements necessary for a more complete analysis of a particular policy issue.

Before we proceed to a discussion of particular policies it will be useful to discuss briefly the economics of damage. First, we shall give a precise definition for the damage caused by a single flood, then we shall give expressions for the expected present value of all future flood damages for any activity. Then, we shall return to discuss various kinds of government action to control flood loss, starting with physical flood protection works. Except for the discussion of flood insurance, we shall assume that the individuals maximize expected monetary value, to avoid the complications of distinguishing between expected utility and EMV. Equivalently we can think of everyone in the flood plain as having flood insurance.

Public policies are often based upon the size of flood damages: some flood relief measures go into effect only if the disaster is declared a "major disaster," estimates of expected damage reduction play a large role in the estimates of benefits of a dam or levee, and flood insurance premiums are based on the amount of damage which is expected to recur.

The Definition of Flood Damage

Conceptually it is fairly clear what we want to know when we ask the meaning of damage: we want to know the economic effect of a particular flood, where by effect we mean the difference between the value of the land taking into account the physical effects of the flood and the value of the land if no flood had taken place. Furthermore, damage should be the cost directly attributable to the flood, not including costs incurred, for example, by inappropriate responses to the flood. Hence, damage should be defined in terms of the value of the optimal investment with the flood, and the optimal investment without the flood. If, for example, after a flood a landowner is uninformed or foolish and chooses an activity which is less valuable than the optimal activity, that loss in value should not be charged off as flood damage, but is properly the cost of misinformation, miscalculation, or foolishness. Similarly, if the flood destroys nonoptimal activities which are then replaced by optimal ones, a direct comparison of the values would underestimate the cost of the flood.

This economic approach to damage leads us to a "with a flood--without a flood" comparison rather than a "before the flood--after the flood" comparison. Before-after comparisons are fundamentally incorrect because they include not only the effects of the flood itself but the effects of anything else that might have happened in the intervening period and the effects of the passage of time. The correct approach to the definition is immediately apparent in the context of optimal replacement as discussed in Chapter 4. After all, within our model, a flood causes a non-optimal replacement. Consider an optimal investment in place with capital equipment of age τ in a flood plain where the value of μ is given. Without a flood we have an expected value of $V(\tau,\mu)$ and with a flood we find ourselves with an expected value of $V(0,\mu)$. The damage suffered as a result of the flood is then simply

(1) $D(\tau,\mu) = V(\tau,\mu) - V(0,\mu)$,

where these are calculated as described in Chapter 4. Recall from Chapter 4 (equation (34)) that

(2) $V(\tau,\mu) = \max [V(\tau,\mu), V(0,\mu)]$

and when $V(\tau,\mu) = V(0,\mu)$, it is time to replace. At that time obviously, damage due to a flood would be zero. Then, the flood would be forcing a change which would have happened in any case.

As an example one can calculate the damage done by a flood to an activity of the "one-hoss shay" type as a function of the age of the capital in place when the flood hits. In the table, damage is expressed as a percentage of a, the initial cost. The other parameters were set arbitrarily ($\rho = .1$, $\mu = .1$, $m = 20$).

τ	Damage	τ	Damage
0.0	1.0	11.0	.85
1.0	.99	12.0	.81
2.0	.99	13.0	.76
3.0	.98	14.0	.71
4.0	.97	15.0	.64
5.0	.96	16.0	.56
6.0	.95	17.0	.45
7.0	.94	18.0	.33
8.0	.92	19.0	.18
9.0	.90	20.0	0.0
10.0	.88		

Indeed, damage declines from 1 to 0 as the capital ages.

In the case when the incumbent activity is not the optimal activity, the damage due to a flood can be calculated in the same manner as the calculation of the optimal replacement policy. If i denotes the incumbent activity and $\tilde{i}$ denotes the optimal activity, the damage caused by a flood when the incumbent activity of age τ is in place is

$$(3) \quad D_i(\tau,\mu) = V_i(\tau,\mu) - V_{\tilde{i}}(0,\mu).$$

If for some reason the incumbent activity has been left in place too long the "damage" to the owner of the land may well be negative. That is, the flood caused a benefit, by forcing a better "decision" than the owner would have voluntarily chosen.

The calculations of $D(\tau,\mu)$ for various benefits streams is complicated. See Brown, Contini and McGuire, 1972, for complete calculations of $D(\tau,\mu)$ for four simple decay patterns. Here we just present the results of those calculations:

No decay:

$$D(\tau,\mu) = a$$

One-hoss shay:

$$D(\tau,\mu) = a \frac{1 - \exp[-(\rho+\mu)(m-\tau)]}{1 - \exp[-m(\rho+\mu)]}$$

Exponential decay:

$$D(\tau,\mu) = a \frac{1 - \exp[-(\rho+\mu)(m-\tau)]}{1 - \exp[-m(\rho+\mu)]} + \frac{b}{\rho+\delta+\mu}\left[e^{-\delta\tau}\{1-\exp[-(\rho+\delta+\mu)(m-\tau)]\} - \frac{\{1-\exp[-(\rho+\mu)(m-\tau)]\}\{1-\exp[(\rho+\delta+\mu)\ m]\}}{\{1-\exp[-(\rho+\mu)\ m]\}}\right]$$

Delayed benefits:

$$D(\tau,\mu) = \begin{cases} a - \frac{b}{\rho+\mu}\exp[-(\rho+\mu)\ \ell] + \frac{b}{\rho} \\ \quad - (\frac{\mu}{\rho+\mu})[\exp[-(\rho+\mu)\cdot(\ell-\tau)] & \text{if} \quad \tau \leq \ell; \\ a + \frac{b}{\rho+\mu}\{1-\exp[-(\rho+\mu)\ell]\}, & \text{if} \quad \tau > \ell. \end{cases}$$

We have shown how to calculate the damage from a single flood at a particular time when the economic activity is completely described and the physical effects of the flood are known. But why is it important to know the damage caused by a flood? Optimal investment decisions in the flood plain are calculated as in Chapters 3 and 4 without reference to damage. Furthermore, as we shall show below, to know the benefits of flood control measures does not require a knowledge of expected damages before or after the flood control measure goes into effect. The concept of damage is useful because that has been made the legal basis for certain kinds of conditional transfers, such as insurance payments or government relief payments. The contract or the law then states that one party shall pay another a certain sum if there is a flood and that sum shall be determined by the amount of damage suffered.

But this kind of contract or law is not necessary. One could also have the amount of payment set in advance or determined by the replacement cost or some other arbitrary rule. There is no obvious a priori reason to choose damage as a basis for these payments.

Now that damage as a function of the age of capital is well defined, the expected present value of damages for any activity can be evaluated. This can be done directly by means of a renewal equation, since damage is a recurring random phenomenon subject to the same probability laws as V_i. We shall call the expected present value of the infinite stream of damages for activity i the hazard cost H_i. H_i can be obtained from the following renewal equation:

$$(4)\quad H_i = \int_0^{\infty} [D_i(T)\, e^{-\rho T} + H_i\, e^{-\rho T}]\, \mu e^{-\mu T}\, dT.$$

The evaluation of (4) for the various types of investment is tedious. Fortunately, there is another way of characterizing the hazard cost which has the double advantage of being conceptually simpler and having an obvious graphical interpretation.

Consider V_i as a function of μ, the flood probability parameter. It is clear that the expected present value of an activity will decrease as the probability of floods increases; that is, V_i is a decreasing function of μ. Figure 5 depicts such a function. $V_i(\mu_o)$ is the expected present value of activity i when it is operated on land where the probability of floods is μ_o. Similarly, $V_i(0)$ is the value of activity i when there will be no floods. The difference between the two is the cost to activity i of a flood hazard of magnitude μ_o. In symbols we have

$$(5)\quad H_i(\mu_o) = V_i(0) - V_i(\mu_o),$$

which is exactly the same as the H_i defined by means of the renewal equation above.

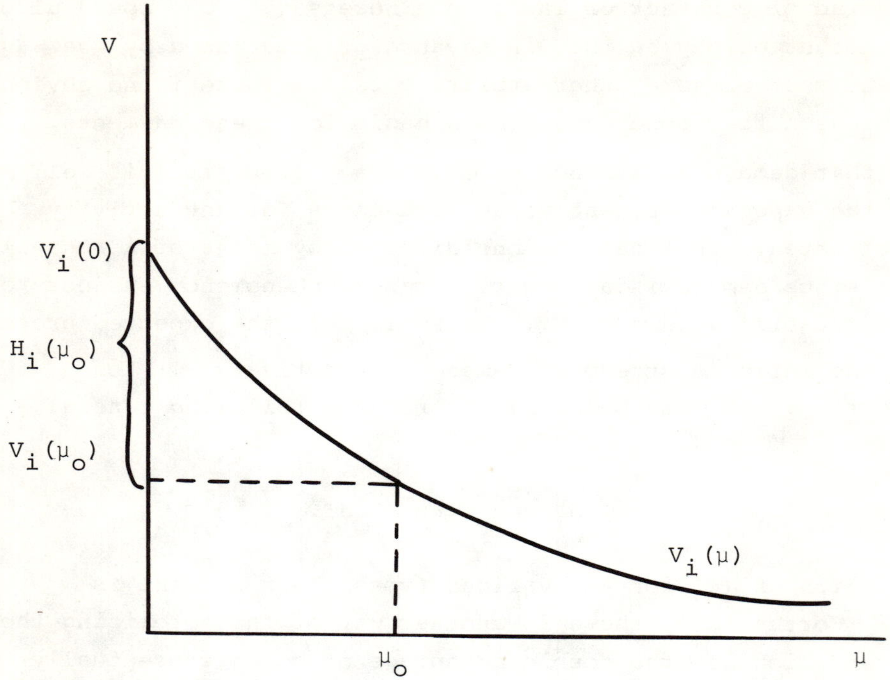

Figure 5

Dams, Levees, and Other Flood Protection Works

Dams, levees, channel clearance and other physical flood protection works benefit the people in the flood plain by reducing the *frequency* or the *severity* of floods or both. For simplicity in our model we have maintained the assumption that floods have a "bang-bang" impact rather than a continuum of possible effects depending, for example, on depth and duration. Thus, we cannot discuss changes in the severity of the impact of a flood for an individual: he is either flooded or not. But the model is sufficiently flexible to handle severity if it is defined as greater or lesser number of acres hit by the flood. Then changes in severity are reflected in changes in the probability of flooding for some of the land on the flood plain.

With this in mind, we turn to a discussion of the economics of physical flood control measures, such as dams or levees, where the measure reduces the probability of floods.[1] We shall not concern ourselves here with the costs of the dam or levee, since that is usually relatively straightforward to calculate. We shall concentrate instead on the benefits derived from reducing flood probabilities. We shall further restrict our focus by disregarding the benefits due to reducing loss of life. We justify such a restriction on two grounds: first, that it is terribly difficult to put a convincing price tag on the value of a human life saved; and second, that floods _per se_ kill remarkably few people compared to the amount of economic damage done, largely because of the warnings usually given to residents of the flood plain.

The benefit to landowners due to reducing the probability of floods is easy to calculate using our model. The benefits (B) are simply the difference between the value of the optimal activity at the higher probability $[V(\mu_2)]$ and the value of the optimal activity at the higher probability $[V(\mu_1)]$, remembering that the optimal activity might change as the flood probability changes. In symbols, we have

$$B \equiv V(\mu_2) - V(\mu_1).$$

Figure 6 illustrates this for two activities, pasture and housing

$$V(\mu_1) = \max\,[V_1(\mu_1), V_2(\mu_1)] = V_1(\mu_1)$$

and

$$V(\mu_2) = \max\,[V_1(\mu_2), V_2(\mu_2)] = V_2(\mu_2)$$

so

$$B = V_2(\mu_2) - V_1(\mu_1).$$

---

[1]This discussion of the effects of reducing flood probabilities is taken from Brown, Contini, and McGuire, 1972.

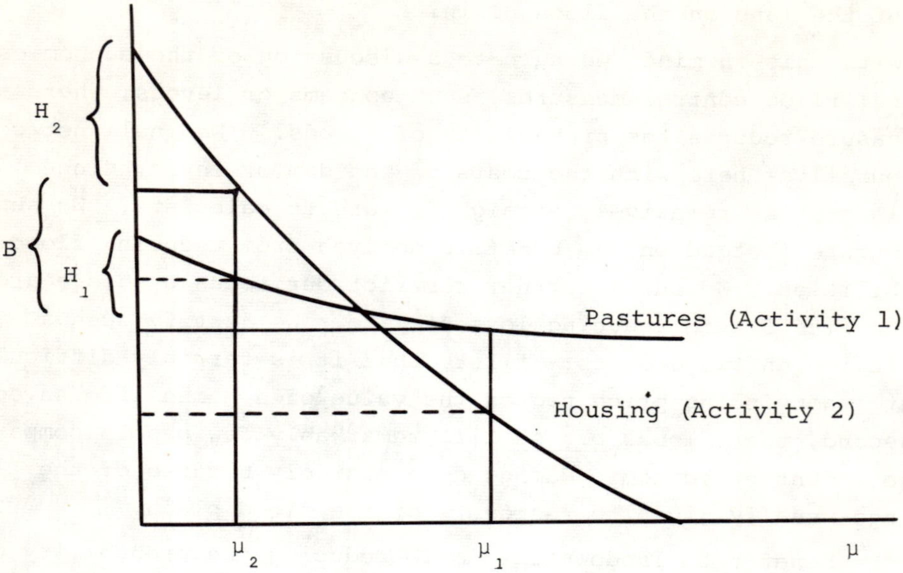

Figure 6

In the figure there are two activities from which to choose. Activity 1, pasture, is hardly vulnerable to floods so that it is more attractive when floods are frequent, that is, when μ is large. The other feasible activity, housing developments, is considerably more vulnerable to floods but is more profitable when floods are infrequent. If the dam were to change the probability of floods on the land from μ_1 to μ_2 the optimal activity would change from pasture to housing. The benefits of the change are, as we noted above, $B = V_2(\mu_2) - V_1(\mu_1)$.

But what has happened to flood damages? In this case they have increased! The expected present value of damages in the original situation was the hazard cost,

$$H_1 = V_1(0) - V_1(\mu_1),$$

and in the new situation it is

$$H_2 = V_2(0) - V_2(\mu_2).$$

Very clearly, H_2 is greater than H_1. The dam will cause average annual damages to increase rather than decrease, even though the benefits of the dam are clearly positive.

This result is not as strange as it might first appear. The goal of the landowner when he responds to the reduction in flood probability is not to reduce damages; his goal is to maximize returns less damages. Often higher returns are accompanied by higher average damages. Only in the case where the optimal activity before and after the dam is the same will the benefit of having the dam be equal to the reduction of damages caused by the flood.

In this formal framework these ideas sound rather trivial. Yet a great deal of effort is spent by government agencies gathering data and estimating damage reduction to be expected as a result of building particular dams. Also there has been much concern in the literature about "flood plain encroachment." It has been observed that even though the government has spent tens of billions of dollars on flood control in the last thirty years, the average annual damage due to floods has not gone down significantly over the period. From our analysis we would not be surprised by this fact. It in no way condemns the government's flood control program nor does it imply irrationality on the part of flood plain residents.

The calculation of expected damage reduction due to the dam is not, by itself, very useful information, except when there will be no change in land use because of the dam. However, estimates of damage reduction can give us lower and upper bounds for the benefits of flood control. The lower bound is the reduction in damage if the incumbent activity (Activity 1) were to remain in place. If we knew what the optimal activity after the dam (Activity 2) were, we could calculate an upper bound on benefits. But then if we know all this, we can calculate benefits directly. In symbols, the bounds on benefits B are as follows:

(1) $DR_1 \leq B \leq DR_2$

where DR denotes damage reduction.

The proof follows directly from the definitions:

$$B = V_2(\mu_2) - V_1(\mu_1),$$

$$(2) \qquad DR_1 = V_1(\mu_2) - V_1(\mu_1),$$

$$DR_2 = V_2(\mu_2) - V_2(\mu_1),$$

and from the implications of optimality,

$$(3) \qquad V_2(\mu_2) \geq V_1(\mu_2)$$

and

$$(4) \qquad V_1(\mu_1) \geq V_2(\mu_1).$$

If we subtract $V_1(\mu_1)$ from both sides of (3) we get

$$(5) \qquad V_2(\mu_2) - V_1(\mu_1) \geq V_1(\mu_2) - V_1(\mu_1)$$

which is, by definition, the first inequality of (1),

$$V \geq DR_1.$$

We get the second inequality of (1) by multiplying (4) by -1, which changes the sense of the inequality, and adding $V_2(\mu_2)$ to get

$$(6) \qquad V_2(\mu_2) - V_1(\mu_1) \leq V_2(\mu_2) - V_2(\mu_1),$$

which is our result:

$$B \leq DR_2.$$

Flood Insurance

In 1968, after fifteen years of work in developing a federal flood insurance program, Congress passed the National Flood Insurance Act of 1968 (Title XII of the Housing and Urban Development Act of 1968). In this section we shall look at some of the theoretical issues raised by the program. We shall start by analyzing the effect of insurance on the individual investor.[2]

[2] This discussion draws mainly on Arrow, 1965.

We shall assume that individuals act to maximize the expected value of utility where utility is a function of income received over time. We shall further assume that in most important economic decisions individuals are risk-averters. That is, given a choice between a lottery with expected monetary value of M and a payment of M with certainty, the individual would prefer the certain payment. From another point of view, we are assuming that the individual does not prefer to gamble and he gets no significant pleasure from the gambling itself.

Assume for a moment that the damages which are incurred because of a flood are well defined and their magnitude, if not their timing, is known in advance. An insurance policy in this case would pay the individual damages if a flood occurs during the year of the contract, and nothing otherwise. In return for assuming this risk, the company would receive a premium. The mathematical expectation of the loss to the insurance company on this policy is simply the product of the flood damages and the probability of a flood. When the premium for the policy is set at pD, the policy is said to be actuarially fair. (Here fair is meant in the sense of fair gamble, not morally fair.) In the language of the act, pD is called the risk premium rate, or the actuarial rate. If insurance is available at actuarially fair rates, then it is clear that risk-averse individuals would buy it; they are made better off by paying the insurance company to take the risk. If the insurance company is not made worse off by selling the policy at an actuarially fair rate, there is a net social gain resulting from the insurance transaction.

Let us look at how a risk-averter's evaluation of an opportunity changes as a result of having insurance available. Consider Figure 7 below. On the vertical axis we measure the individual's certainty monetary equivalent, that is, the amount of money that he would be willing to pay for the opportunity of operating the activity indefinitely. On the horizontal axis we put the flood parameter μ, as usual.

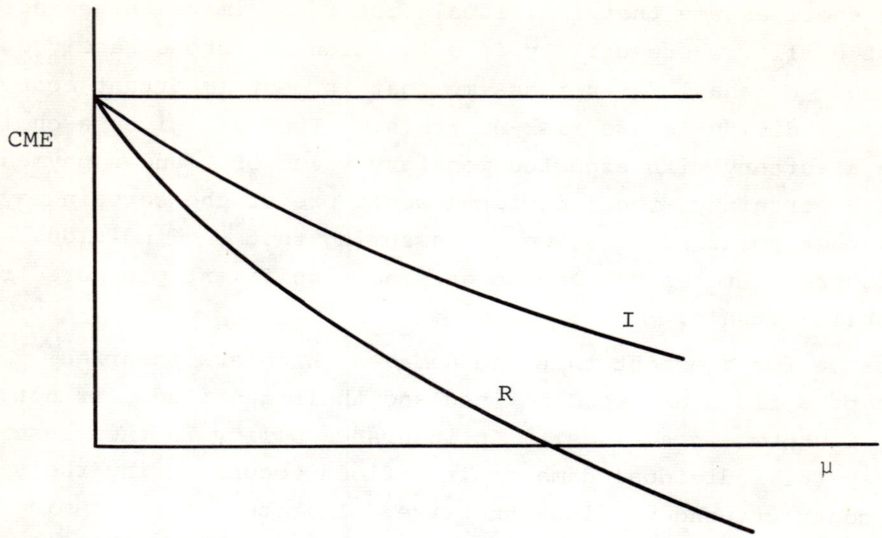

Figure 7

The curve marked I (for insured) is the expected present monetary value of the activity as a function of μ. Insurance will pay for any costs associated with flooding. Therefore, it gives the activity a certain value of $V(0)$ regardless of the value taken by μ, on the payment of a premium. This premium increases with the hazard and is exactly the difference between $V(0)$ and I for any value of μ. The curve marked R gives the certainty monetary equivalent of $V(\mu)$ for a risk-averse individual. When μ is zero there is no risk and the two evaluations are equal. As μ increases, the risk inherent in the activity increases and the two evaluations diverge. This divergence, of course, measures the value to the individual of insurance, since insurance changes a risky venture into a riskless one.

Let us look at the transaction from the point of view of the insurance company. If there is a large number of statistically independent risks in its portfolio, then by the Law of Large Numbers it is practically certain that the amount lost by the company in any one year will be very close to the mathematical expectation. Its risk is drastically diminished by pooling. At actuarially fair rates the insurance company will usually come very close to breaking even. When there is a loading charge, that is, when the rate is above pD, the insurance company with a large number of independent risks can expect almost certainly to make a profit. If the loading charge is less than the amount that the individual is willing to pay to avoid risks, the transaction will make both parties better off. Again, there is a net social gain.

The lack of insurance can lead to a misallocation of resources, as is easily shown in Figure 8.

If insurance is available, the decision maker will choose Activity 1 if the value of μ is below μ^*. If no insurance is available, and the decision maker is risk-averse, he would choose the risky Activity 1 only if μ took a value of less than μ'.

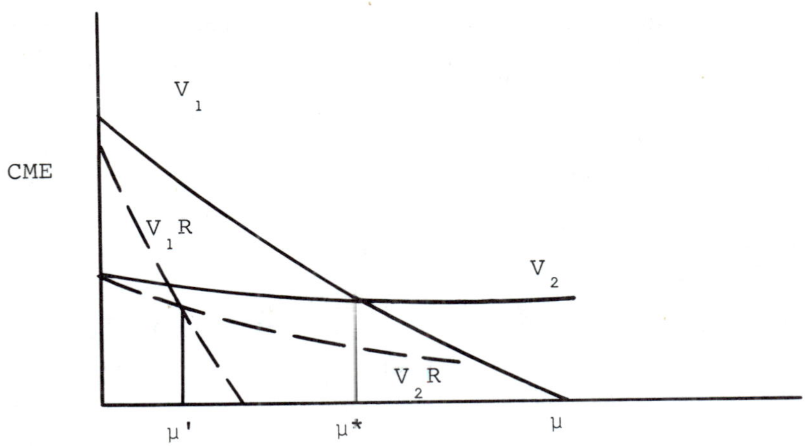

Figure 8

Then in the case for values of μ between μ' and μ^*, the more conservative Activity 2 will be chosen over Activity 1 even though 1 would be better from (risk-neutral) society's point of view. The possibility of shifting risks allows people to engage in risky activities they would otherwise avoid. Of course, there will still be flood losses, but insurance relieves the individual decision maker of their impact, except for the insurance premium, which is the social cost of the risk.

But the trading of risks is only part of what interests us here. The financial ability to bear risk and the entrepreneurial ability to operate activities which are particularly appropriate in some flood plain are quite unlikely to appear in the same person. Good farmers are often not good financiers. Yet risks are inherent in operating in a flood plain. If there is no method of sharing or trading risks, then farmers will be prevented from working good bottom land unless they are able to finance the occasional losses that will occur. Thus the ability to shift risks, as with insurance, makes it possible for individuals to undertake risky ventures that they would otherwise be unable to bear. There are other methods to share risk besides insurance. The stock market is one example: it allows an industrialist to engage in risky productive activities even when he could not afford to run the risk of failure, since bankruptcy laws limit his liability and thereby shift the risks onto creditors. Methods of shifting risk which are more germane to the case at hand are relief and charity. When catastrophe strikes, the community at large steps in to offer help; it is willing to share part of the risk. In the case of floods this has been a very important method of risk spreading. Over the years it has become apparent that it is socially and politically intolerable for flood risks to be borne entirely by the occupants of the flood plain. The federal disaster relief role has grown steadily, even though the amount spent on flood control programs has grown to be very large. In fact, to a large extent it is because of the growing costs of flood relief programs that the government has decided to enter into a flood insurance program. A flood insurance program would eliminate federal responsibility for flood relief and provide a more efficient and equitable way of sharing the risks in a flood plain.

Let us look at exactly how flood insurance would work in our model. For simplicity we shall assume throughout our discussion that premium rates are actuarially fair. Consider first a world with discrete time intervals of a year. Then a one-year insurance contract would be easily defined. The loss sustained because of a flood would be the difference between the expected present value of the activity if a flood occurred and the expected present value of the activity if a flood did not occur (recall that the expected present value would include all cash flows such as rebuilding, clean-up, etc.). This is the amount that the insurance company would pay if a flood occurred. For that contract the insured would pay a premium which would be equal to the probability of a flood in a year multiplied by the amount the insurance company would have to pay if the flood did occur (assume actuarially fair rates). To find the continuous premium rate, reduce the length of the contract to an instant in the limit.

Let μ take a particular known value, say μ^*. We showed earlier that the present value of damages to an activity operated forever in a flood plain where the flood hazard is constant over time is simply the difference between the actual value of the activity and its expected present value if there were no floods. Symbolically, if A is the present value of the damage stream, then

$$A = V(0) - V(\mu^*).$$

If the premium were to be constant over time, it would simply be at a rate whose present value were A, that is ρA. The present value of the receipts expected from operating the activity and from the insurance policy total $V(\mu^*) + A = V(0)$. The amount to be paid for the policy is the present value of the premiums $\rho A/\rho = A$. Thus, the net worth of the activity and the insurance policy associated with it is $V(0) - A = V(\mu^*)$.

The availability of insurance causes the individual to evaluate the activity at its expected present value, regardless of his own feelings of risk aversion. Because the government is so large compared to the projects under consideration, it, too, is risk-neutral and evaluates opportunities at their expected value. Thus, the availability of insurance to the individual on a voluntary basis brings the individual's view of risk into line with the government's view. If the individual were risk-averse he would want to buy the insurance; if he were risk-neutral he would be indifferent toward the insurance. We have assumed away the problem of riskophiles.

John V. Krutilla has advocated a federal flood insurance program which was slightly different from that finally enacted; he proposed that insurance be compulsory.[3] In his article he pointed out that the net effect of flood control legislation has been to cause flood damage potential to <u>increase</u> even after $6 billion has been spent. This result is not surprising, nor is it necessarily bad--if one keeps in mind that the purpose of flood control is not to reduce flood damages but to increase the benefits from the flood plain net of damages. The increase in flood damages is a problem mainly because the government has found itself forced to take increasing responsibility for the damages, while the private sector has kept the rewards when the floods do not occur. People, Krutilla notes, tend to move into the flood plain in response to flood control. This seems to indicate that the activity mix in the flood plain changes with a reduction in the flood hazard, just as one would predict from our model.

In the same article Krutilla claims that the reduction in flood insurance premiums (which is equivalent to the reduction in damages) would measure the benefits from a dam or levee. This would be the case only if there were no change in activity due to the structure. However, it is at least true that the reduction in damages measured as if there were no change in activity is a lower bound to the benefits if there is a change, for a change will be made <u>only</u> if the landowner is benefited by it.

An extreme proposal has been made which would have the government bear <u>all</u> losses due to floods. The individual would simply send a bill to the government for all losses incurred as a result of the flood. When combined with special taxes on houses or on real estate, this program has been called "flood insurance."[4] Clearly this is a misnomer. The costs borne by the individual bear no relationship to the risk incurred; the scheme is simply a real estate

---

[3]Krutilla, 1966.

[4]U. S. Congress, Senate, 1966, p. 38.

tax combined with a subsidy to those who invest in risky areas. Furthermore, the subsidy increases with the risk. This is hardly good social policy. It would be inequitable and would encourage people to take advantage of the subsidy by building in hazardous areas. This would be reasonable for the individual to do because he would not bear the hazard. Clearly, such a program would encourage inefficient use of the land. Consider the diagram in Figure 9.

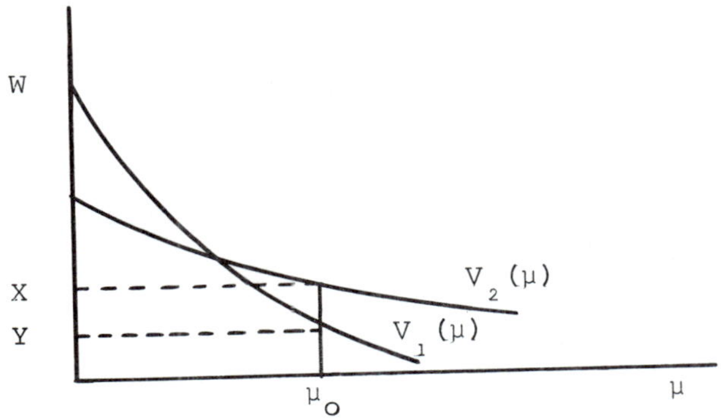

Figure 9

We have displayed the value of two activities as a function of the flood probability parameter, μ, as calculated in Chapter 3. The values of the activities are net of the premium-tax which would have to be paid in the scheme under discussion. Activity 1 is relatively risky and Activity 2 is relatively secure, so 1 is preferable when flood risks are low and 2 when they are high. Let the flood parameter take a value of μ_o. Then the optimal activity is 2 with value X. From the point of view of the individual, though, his criterion is simply to choose the activity which would be best if there were <u>no</u> floods. In this case that is Activity 1, which he evaluates at W. The amount that he can expect to earn by operating Activity 1 is only Y, but the government's damage payments would make up the difference between W and Y. If he could be induced to choose Activity 2, the loss to the government would be considerably less, the difference between X and Y.[5] Thus, the effect of such a plan would be to encourage a misallocation of resources in favor of high risk investments, at the same time leading to large transfer payments from the government to the individuals who choose to misallocate the resources.

Flood Relief

Relief funds are usually available to the owners of business and private property located in the flood plain. Relief may come in different forms.[6] In some cases, namely when public facilities are destroyed, the Office of Emergency Planning is authorized to call upon federal agencies to assist in the restoration work and share the expenses. The Bureau of Public Roads provides similar help when roads are damaged (whether they are county, state or federal roads). The Small Business Administration provides rehabilitation loans on very favorable terms to private property owners and small businesses. The American Red Cross, the Department of Agriculture and several other agencies often participate in relief for flood-struck areas. The Internal Revenue Service allows a deduction on flood damages for several years after the damage has occurred.

Our intention here is to explore how relief policies differ in their effect. From a purely conceptual viewpoint, all relief policies can be considered in the same simplified fashion: an outright monetary payment made after the flood, proportionate to the damage or, more often, to the reconstruction costs.[7] We shall limit our discussion to such an idealized refund policy. However, our

---

[5]To be consistent with the earlier presentation, and to make the premiums and damage payments consistent with activity evaluations, we have converted everything into present value terms. Thus, when we say premium in the text we mean the discounted present value of an infinite stream of annual premium payments.

[6]All the various government disaster relief programs are described in detail in the appendices to U. S. Congress, Senate, 1966.

[7]For instance, a reconstruction loan on very favorable terms can be considered as an outright money payment. This payment is the difference between the present values of the loan at the low rate and the same loan at the market rate of interest.

conclusions can be generalized for more complicated cases.

Let us consider the following simple refund policy. Immediately after each flood each private landowner in the flood plain will be paid by the government a percentage k of the reconstruction cost, the percentage to be an exponentially declining function of the age of the capital in place when the flood hit, τ. The relief payment is then given by $R_i(\tau) = a_i k e^{-\gamma\tau}$, where $0 \leq k \leq 1$, and $\gamma \geq 0$. If a flood occurs while the capital is in place the landowner receives a relief payment from the government according to this formula.

If the replacement age for each activity is given and is denoted by m_i, then the expected value of the relief payment from the first flood if it happens in the first m_i years is

$$E_\mu(R_i) = \int_0^{m_i} a_i \; k e^{-(\gamma - \rho)T} \mu e^{-\mu T} \, dT \qquad i = 1, \ldots, n$$

$$= \frac{a_i k \mu}{\gamma + \rho + \mu} \left(1 - e^{-(\gamma + \rho + \mu)m_i}\right).$$

The expected value of all future relief payments when activity i is operated indefinitely is

$$V_\mu(R_i) = E_\mu(R_i) + E_\mu \; e^{-\rho T} \; V_\mu(R_i)$$

$$= E_\mu(R_i) + \frac{\mu}{\rho + \mu} \; V_\mu(R_i)$$

$$= \frac{\rho + \mu}{\rho} \; E_\mu R_i$$

$$= a_i \, k \left(\frac{\mu}{\rho}\right) \left(\frac{\rho + \mu}{\gamma + \rho + \mu}\right) \left(1 - e^{-(\gamma + \rho + \mu)m_i}\right).$$

It is clear from this that $V_\mu R$ increases, <u>ceteris paribus</u>, with a, μ, and m_i. That is, the subsidy involved in the relief payment favors high capital intensity (high a), high risk (high μ) and longer-lived investments (high m_i).

The effect can be seen in Figure 10. For simplicity of calculation, consider two activities of the no-decay variety. Without any relief, we have

$$V_1 = \frac{b_1}{\rho} - a_1 \left(\frac{\rho + \mu}{\rho}\right)$$

$$V_2 = \frac{b_2}{\rho} - a_2 \left(\frac{\rho + \mu}{\rho}\right).$$

When the government provides relief according to the above formula, the landowner evaluates each activity according to

$$VR_1 = V_1 + a_1 k \left(\frac{\mu}{\rho}\right) \left(\frac{\rho + \mu}{\gamma + \rho + \mu}\right)$$

$$VR_2 = V_2 + a_2 k \left(\frac{\mu}{\rho}\right) \left(\frac{\rho + \mu}{\gamma + \rho + \mu}\right). \qquad (m_1 = m_2 = \infty)$$

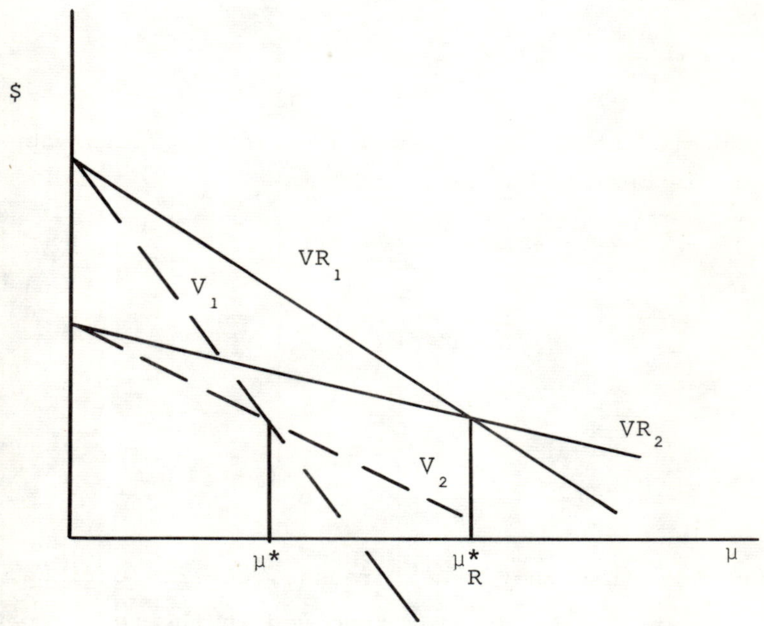

Figure 10

In the figure, dashed lines denote V's, full lines denote VR's. The vertical distance between V_1 and VR_1 at any μ is the expected value of the relief payments. Without relief, the landowner chooses Activity 1 if μ is less than μ^*. With relief, however, he will choose Activity 1 as long as μ is less than μ^*_R. It is clear then that instituting relief payments will change the choice of activity in at least part of the flood plain.

The next question is: Is that good? In general, we would expect not. To reason this out we have to have a "social" criterion for the allocation of flood plain lands. Then we can rephrase our question as follows: "Does V or VR more closely approximate the socially optimal use of the land?" A simple rule to adopt as a social criterion would be the maximization of private expected monetary value. We use the private value because we can legitimately assume away any differences between private and social costs; we are not concerned here with externalities. We use expected <u>monetary</u> value because the possible losses due to floods are such a small part of the nation's wealth that social risk aversion here is nil (see page 7 above) and, therefore, expected social utility is directly proportional to expected monetary value.

If the private landowner is insured against floods or is risk neutral, he will maximize expected monetary value in the absence of a relief program. In other words, his decisions based on the pre-relief valuation (V) will be optimal. If the institution of a relief program changes his decisions, the effect of this program will be a misallocation of resources. There is also a question of income redistribution here. A relief policy would transfer income from taxpayers to landowners in flood plains in proportion to the amount at risk. Such a redistribution of income cannot be easily justified.

If the landowner is risk averse, his evaluation of the various activities, in the absence of a relief policy, will be less than the social evaluation, and he will tend to allocate the land to less risky investments, such as Activity 2 in Figure 10. His private criterion, μ^*, in other words, would be farther to the left than the social μ^*. The availability of relief payments would cause him to move his criterion in the direction of the social criterion.

However, we cannot know in advance how far it would move. Furthermore, if there is a market for the land with known μ and if the same activities are available to all, the less risk-averse people would be able to bid the land away from the more risk-averse. Thus, the potential beneficial effects of the policy might never be realized, since the people whom the government intends to help would be bid out of the market. The effect of the relief policy would then be to subsidize risk-neutral people for taking risks. Again, such a redistribution cannot be easily justified.

Flood Plain Zoning

Flood plain zoning is an increasingly important tool for policy-makers who have to deal with rising claims from flood damage. The theory which we have developed in the chapters above makes clear the uses and impact of flood plain zoning. At its simplest, zoning is a rule of the form: "Thou shalt not..." It reduces the number of options available to the landowner. He must choose from a restricted set of activities--those which are legal--rather than from the set of all technologically feasible activities. The justifications for flood plain zoning are fundamentally the same as for any other constraints by a society on its members: the individual should be protected from his own folly or ignorance, or the rest of society should be protected from acts by the individual which infringe upon others.

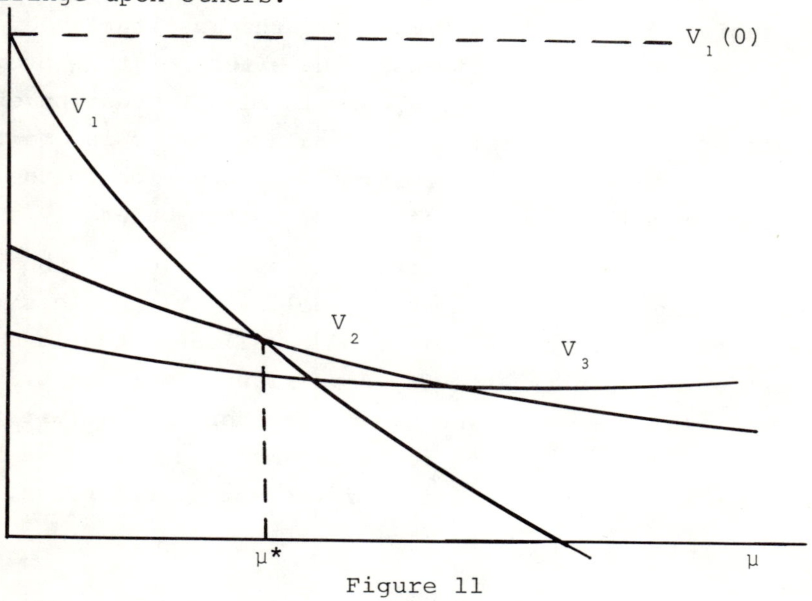

Figure 11

Figure 11 illustrates a situation which we shall use in our discussion of flood plain zoning. There are three feasible activities. Activity 1, housing, is the most risky and is against the zoning code. The others are less risky agricultural activities. In a world where the individual and the zoning board (society) have complete knowledge of Figure 11, and they both know the true value for μ (as in Chapter 2), and there are no external effects when housing is flooded (the neighbors do not bear any costs when a house is flooded), a zoning ordinance against housing is either irrelevant or wrong, depending on the true value of μ. If μ is greater than μ^*, then the individual would not choose to build housing in the first place, so the zoning restriction is irrelevant. Only if μ takes a value less than μ^* does the zoning law have an effect. It prevents him from choosing the activity which he prefers. Thus zoning hurts the landowner and does not benefit the rest of society.

Yet, if this is the case, why is flood plain zoning so often discussed and practiced? A variety of reasons have been suggested,[8] all having to do with relaxation in the conditions set forth in the paragraph above. We shall discuss the suggested justifications for zoning, one by one.

Zoning is often justified by pointing to the ignorance of individual landowners. They might not know the effect of a flood on their property; or they might not know the probability of a flood (the case which we discussed in Chapter 5); or they might simply be irrational in the sense of not believing that floods could happen to them; or they might be neurotic in the sense that they are not able to face and prepare for the horrible possibility of a flood. If the individual does not know the effect of a flood on his land--that it will damage or destroy his housing--he will evaluate housing as if there were no floods, that is, by the horizontal line at $V_1(0)$ in Figure 11. The landowner would clearly choose Activity 1, whatever value is taken by μ. Then a zoning prohibition would be socially useful if the true value of μ were greater than μ^*. A

---

[8] See Pendleton, 1967.

more subtle and preferable policy would be to inform the landowner about the damage that floods can cause. A particularly effective way of informing him might be to have lending agencies require that all borrowers buy flood insurance. Similarly, flood plain zoning would be sensible if the authorities know the probability of floods, but the individual does not.[9] There are a couple of cases where one would expect that the community would have better estimates of the flood probability than the individual: first, if the community had access to expertise in hydrology; and second, if the community was likely to have greater experience than the individual, as would be the case in tract developments. Again, a simpler and, insofar as decentralized decisions are good, a better policy would be to inform the community about the potential hazard.[10] Again, flood insurance would serve this purpose quite well. A flood insurance program would make the landowner aware that floods were a hazard and would inform him of the government's estimate of μ.

If, however, neither the authorities nor the individual have very good ideas about what the true value of μ is, then there is no prior reason to assume that the government is right and the individual is wrong. What if the opposite were true? Then the government would be protecting its ignorance and harming the individual.

There is little that economists can say about irrational or neurotic decision making except that it is expensive and painful; hopefully it is not necessary to base a flood plain policy on anticipated delusions and neuroses. If this were the case, however, it would still not be obvious *a priori* why the zoning board would be free of the same delusions and neuroses.

Another group of justifications for flood plain zoning has to do with externalities caused by certain activities. In the case of

---

[9]From the point of view of Chapter 5, we would say that his beliefs about the flood process are such that his prior distribution of μ has a small t parameter; that is, it is as if he had observed the process for only a very short length of time.

[10]See White, 1964, for a discussion of the practical difficulties in this seemingly simple policy.

flood plain zoning the externalities are usually of the sort that increases the flood hazard up or down stream. In this case the social evaluation of an activity is different from the private. Costs are incurred by other landowners as a result of decisions to which they were not party and for which they are not compensated. Unless more subtle means of compensation can be designed to protect the interests of the injured third parties, some sort of blunt prohibition may be necessary. Even here, though, the zoning board must weigh the benefits to the owner against the costs to the third party before it can wisely use its powers of prohibition.

If society accepts the responsibility for some of the risks of flooding, as when it provides flood relief, then it has the right to limit its responsibility, by regulating the amount of risk which individuals may take. Zoning is a crude method of achieving that end. Flood insurance obviates the need for society to take responsibility for some of the risks, and should remove the need for the flood plain zoning based on this responsibility.

Unfortunately, Title III of the Federal Flood Insurance Program is designed to encourage local "land management programs" which include flood zoning. Furthermore, flood insurance is to be available only in communities which have assured the government that "permanent land use and control measures have been adopted" and will be enforced. This seems to be a rather retrogressive part of an otherwise very progressive act by the government. There seems to be very little justification for flood plain zoning when there is an active flood insurance program. To make zoning a precondition of insurance seems to be mistaken, except where the zoning is explicitly intended to prevent damage to third parties.

CHAPTER 7

COMPUTER SIMULATION OF INVESTMENT BEHAVIOR IN A FLOOD PLAIN

There is a large and growing body of literature describing experiments in computer simulation of river basins.[1] The reasons for this lie in the vast complications of designing and operating a water resource system. The complexities are such that analytic methods have been insufficient to cope with the problem, but large-scale computers can be used to model the manifold possibilities and then run the model through a large number of histories and see which design and operating rules work best.

Typically, the simulations have been done with an eye to closely modeling the engineering and hydrological features of the system while leaving the economic feature in a broad brush state. I have done just the opposite. I have concentrated on the economics of the situation and have left the hydrological and technical aspects very crude. An enormous amount of programming effort is required to design simulations so I decided not to concern myself with that, but instead to concern myself with modeling the investment decision aspects of the program rather than the hydrologic and technical aspects.

To illustrate the practical workings of the model developed in this paper, a computer simulation program has been written. As input, the program accepts descriptions of the payoff streams of a set of activities. The activities can be of the no-decay, one-hoss shay, or exponential decay type. As output, the program calculates the expected present value (V) for each of the activities and selects the best one for values of μ ranging from 0.01 to 1.00, and plots V against the return period (recall that the return period for a flood is $1/\mu$). Then, the program simulates the history of a piece of land in a flood plain where the owner follows an adaptive policy, choosing the activity which would be best if his current estimate of μ were correct. In effect, we

---

[1]See Maass, et. al., 1962, Hufschmidt and Fiering, 1966, Fiering, 1967, Loucks, et. al., 1969.

are simulating the intermediate case of Chapter 5.

At the beginning of a particular history the landowner has beliefs about the true value of μ, and those beliefs are described by the two parameters of a γ distribution (JRZERO, TZERO). For his initial investment he chooses that activity (MAXACT) which would have the highest present value if $\mu = r/t$ (JRZERO/TZERO). Then, a random number generator gives a random number which is transformed through a negative exponential distribution with the true value of μ as parameter, resulting in the date of the next flood (TFLOOD). The computer then goes to the date the activity in place expires or TFLOOD, whichever comes first. Then, the landowner collects that part of the payment stream of MAXACT which is his due, denoted $W_i^*(T)$ in Chapter 2, and discounts it back to time zero. At the same time he adjusts his beliefs about μ, taking into account what he has learned about μ since the last update. This is done by simply adding the appropriate numbers to his priors (JRZERO and TZERO). Based on his new estimate of μ he chooses the activity which would have the highest expected present value (MAXACT). So the process goes until the history is complete (TSTOP).

When the history is complete, a new history is generated until the desired number of histories for the sample (J) is reached. Then, the average present value of the sample (EPVBAR) is calculated. This is an estimate of the expected present value of following the decision rule given above, conditional on the true value of μ. In the program the choice of the true μ is a random choice, chosen from the γ distribution which describes the landowner's initial prior distribution. The program chooses I different values for μ, repeating the whole process each time. The average present value over all the samples (EPVUNC) is then computed. This is the estimate of the unconditional expected present value for the initial prior distribution.

The situation of Chapter 2, where the landowner knows the true value of μ, can be simulated by letting I be one and letting the initial priors be so large that the amount of experience he gets will not change the estimate of μ significantly.

A sample of the program output makes clear the operation of the program. Figure 12 is a print-out of the first part of the program, which calculates the expected present value of five activities as a function of μ. The five activities are of the one-hoss shay variety, having the following initial costs and benefit stream parameters:

Activity	Initial Cost	Benefit	Life
1	10	2	15
2	4	1	10
3	25	15	2
4	100	15	15
5	0	0	1

The actual numbers chosen have no particular significance; they are intended only as examples. The fifth activity is to be interpreted as leaving the land fallow, checking every year whether or not to continue to leave it fallow. From the print-out we see that leaving the land fallow is the best policy if μ is greater than approximately .15. Then, as the probability of a flood declines, activities 2, 3, and 4 come into favor in that order.

Figure 13 gives an example of a simulated history, history 5 of sample 3 in this case. The true value of μ, unknown to the landowner, is 0.0231. The landowner's initial estimate, for whatever reasons, is 0.1, so he is overly pessimistic about the flood process. That is, the landowner expects floods to recur about every ten years, whereas in fact they have a return period of every 44 years.

If the true μ were known the landowner would choose activity 4, the most floodprone activity, and could expect to earn approximately \$56.05. Instead, because his estimate of μ is so pessimistic, he chooses activity 3, a more conservative activity. It has an expected present value of \$6.56 if he had estimated μ properly.

μ	Return	V(1)	V(2)	V(3)	V(4)	V(5)	VMAX	MAXACT
1.000	1.000	-143.333	-54.002	-251.912	-1516.666	0.0	0.0	5
0.500	2.000	-60.021	-20.805	-96.336	-683.543	0.0	0.0	5
0.333	3.000	-32.402	-10.079	-50.913	-407.356	0.0	0.0	5
0.250	4.000	-18.832	-4.975	-29.548	-271.655	0.0	0.0	5
0.200	5.000	-10.895	-2.057	-17.174	-192.286	0.0	0.0	5
0.167	6.000	-5.749	-0.192	-9.111	-140.821	0.0	0.0	5
0.143	7.000	-2.170	1.095	-3.445	-105.030	0.0	1.095	2
0.125	8.000	0.450	2.032	0.753	-78.836	0.0	2.032	2
0.111	9.000	2.443	2.744	3.989	-58.906	0.0	3.989	3
0.100	10.000	4.006	3.302	6.558	-43.272	0.0	6.558	3
0.091	11.000	5.263	3.750	8.648	-30.700	0.0	8.648	3
0.083	12.000	6.295	4.118	10.381	-20.384	0.0	10.381	3
0.077	13.000	7.156	4.425	11.840	-11.775	0.0	11.840	3
0.071	14.000	7.885	4.686	13.087	-4.487	0.0	13.087	3
0.067	15.000	8.509	4.909	14.165	1.760	0.0	14.165	3
0.063	16.000	9.050	5.103	15.104	7.171	0.0	15.104	3
0.059	17.000	9.524	5.273	15.932	11.903	0.0	15.932	3
0.056	18.000	9.941	5.422	16.666	16.074	0.0	16.666	3
0.053	19.000	10.311	5.555	17.321	19.778	0.0	19.778	4
0.050	20.000	10.642	5.674	17.910	23.088	0.0	23.088	4
0.048	21.000	10.940	5.781	18.442	26.064	0.0	26.064	4
0.045	22.000	11.209	5.878	18.925	28.754	0.0	28.754	4
0.043	23.000	11.453	5.966	19.365	31.196	0.0	31.196	4
0.042	24.000	11.676	6.047	19.769	33.424	0.0	33.424	4
0.040	25.000	11.880	6.120	20.139	35.464	0.0	35.464	4
0.038	26.000	12.067	6.188	20.481	37.338	0.0	37.338	4
0.037	27.000	12.240	6.250	20.797	39.067	0.0	39.067	4
0.036	28.000	12.400	6.308	21.090	40.666	0.0	40.666	4
0.034	29.000	12.548	6.362	21.363	42.149	0.0	42.149	4
0.033	30.000	12.686	6.412	21.617	43.529	0.0	43.529	4
0.032	31.000	12.815	6.458	21.855	44.816	0.0	44.816	4
0.031	32.000	12.935	6.502	22.078	46.019	0.0	46.019	4
0.030	33.000	13.048	6.543	22.287	47.145	0.0	47.145	4
0.029	34.000	13.154	6.581	22.484	48.203	0.0	48.203	4
0.029	35.000	13.253	6.617	22.670	49.197	0.0	49.197	4
0.028	36.000	13.347	6.651	22.844	50.134	0.0	50.134	4
0.027	37.000	13.435	6.684	23.010	51.018	0.0	51.018	4
0.026	38.000	13.519	6.714	23.167	51.854	0.0	51.854	4
0.026	39.000	13.598	6.743	23.315	52.646	0.0	52.646	4
0.025	40.000	13.673	6.770	23.457	53.396	0.0	53.396	4
0.024	41.000	13.744	6.796	23.591	54.108	0.0	54.108	4
0.024	42.000	13.812	6.821	23.719	54.786	0.0	54.786	4

Figure 12

Sample, History 3 5			Reward		
μ Estimate	Date	Act;	-Dry	-Flood	Value so Far
0.1000	0.0	3	3.27		3.27
0.0833	2.000	3		-3.53	0.14
0.1482	3.497	2	3.52		2.99
0.0851	13.497	3	3.27		4.45
0.0784	15.497	3	3.27		5.74
0.0727	17.497	3	3.27		6.88
0.0678	19.497	3	3.27		7.90
0.0625	21.497	3	3.27		8.80
0.0597	23.497	3	3.27		9.60
0.0563	25.497	3	3.27		10.31
0.0533	27.497	4	48.36		19.59
0.0381	42.497	4	48.36		23.37
0.0296	57.497	4		-61.83	21.41
0.0427	60.258	4	48.36		22.71
0.0352	75.258	4	48.36		23.24
0.0299	90.258	4		10.65	23.28

Sample Over. Expected P.V. 36.488 Conditional on μ = 0.0231

Figure 13

Now let us look at the simulation print-out more carefully. Each line gives us the estimate of μ at a particular date, the action chosen at that date, the reward generated by that act until the next decision date, and the contribution that the reward makes to the present value discounted back to time zero. The first line tells us that at date zero the landowner estimated μ to be 0.10 and he chose activity 3, which was in place for its full two years (until the date of the next line), earning a reward of $3.27. From the second line we see that as a result of his experience in the first two years he adjusts his estimate of μ downward, now to 0.0833. This is not sufficiently low for him to change his choice of activity, so he again chooses activity 3.

This time a flood comes at year 3.497, before the life of the activity is up. As a result the landowner loses $3.53, which is worth $3.13 discounted back to zero. The flood causes the landowner to become more pessimistic and adjust his estimate of μ upwards to 0.14. That, in turn, leads him to choose a more conservative investment, activity 2. The next flood is not to appear until year 60. In the meantime the landowner is becoming more optimistic about the flood process and his estimate is approaching the true value. The flood in the sixtieth year slows this process down. Notice that a loss of \$61 at year 60 is discounted to just under \$2.00 at time zero, using an interest rate of six per cent. The history is terminated at 100 years after having earned \$23.28 in present value.

Since this was the last history in the sample, the next line tells us that the expected present value conditional on μ being 0.0231 is \$36.49. This is the mean value over the sample drawn with this value of μ.

It is obvious from the sample history that the present value converges over time due to the interest rate; the impact of whatever happens late in the history is greatly diminished by discounting. The difference in present values among histories in the same sample is largely due to random differences in the early part of the histories.

Since we are interested in how much is learned as well as how much is earned, we should also consider what happens to the estimate of μ as time goes on. In our example where $\mu = .0231$, the landowner had revised his estimate of μ from .10 to .0299, over the 90 year history. Thus his estimate of μ had improved sufficiently for him to be choosing the correct activity (no. 4) even though he was still somewhat too pessimistic about the true μ. It should be noted that the flood parameter estimate does not converge as fast as does the present value. That is simply because it is a much slower process. Only after a very long time would the current estimate of μ become insensitive to random floods.

The speed of convergence is obviously determined by the size of the true μ. In a hundred years one can learn all one needs to know about a flood process where floods come on an average of every two years, but when floods are less frequent, as in our example, a hundred years is not sufficient necessarily to get a good estimate of μ.

REFERENCES

Arrow, Kenneth J., Aspects of the Theory of Risk-bearing, Yrjo Jahnsson Lectures, Helsinki, 1965.

Arrow, Kenneth J., "Criteria for Social Investment," Water Resources Research, 1, 1, 1965.

Arrow, Kenneth J. and Mordecai Kurz, Public Investment, the Rate of Return, and Optimal Fiscal Policy, Resources for the Future, Washington, 1970.

Baumol, W. J., "On the Social Rate of Discount," The American Economic Review, 58, 4, September, 1968, 788-802.

Beckmann, Martin, Dynamic Programming of Economic Decisions, Berlin, New York: Springer-Verlag, 1968.

Bellman, Richard, Dynamic Programming, Santa Monica, California: RAND Corporation, 1956.

Bhattacharjee, Manish C., "Optimal Investment in the Face of Floods," Working Paper 259, Center for Research in Management Science, University of California, Berkeley, 1968.

Bhavnagri, V. S. and G. Bugliarello, "Flood Proofing in a Flood Plain: A Stochastic Model," Proceedings of American Society of Civil Engineers, 92,HY4, 63-76, July, 1966.

Bhavnagri, V. S. and G. Bugliarello, "Mathematical Model of an Urban Flood Plain," Proceedings of American Society of Civil Engineers, 91, HY2, 149-174, March, 1965.

Blackwell, David, "Discounted Dynamic Programming," Annals of Mathematical Statistics, 36, 226-235, 1965.

Blackwell, David, "Positive Dynamic Programming," Proceedings of the Fifth Berkeley Symposium on Mathematical Statistics and Probability, Vol. I, 415-418, Berkeley and Los Angeles: University of California Press, 1967.

Borch, Karl, The Economics of Uncertainty, Princeton: Princeton University Press, 1968.

Brown, John P., Bruno Contini, and C. B. McGuire, "An Economic Model of Flood Plain Land Use and Land Use Policy," Water Resources Research, February, 1972.

Buchlin, Stanley, Computer Programs for the Analysis of Complex Decision Problems, Harvard Business School, 1969.

Burton, Ian, Types of Agricultural Occupance of Flood Plains in the United States, Department of Geography, Research Paper No. 75, Chicago: University of Chicago Press, 1962.

Cord, Joel, "A Method for Allocating Funds to Investment Projects when Returns are Subject to Uncertainty," Management Science, 335-341, January, 1964.

Cox, D. R. and P. A. W. Lewis, The Statistical Analysis of Series of Events, London: Methuen & Co., 1966.

Eckstein, Otto, Water Rescurce Development: The Economics of Project Evaluation, Cambridge: Harvard University Press, 1958.

Edwards, Ward and Amos Tversky, eds., Decision Making; Selected Readings, Baltimore: Penguin Books, 1967.

Epstein, B., "Test for the Validity of the Assumption that the Underlying Distribution of Life is Exponential," Technometrics, 2, 1, 1960, pp. 83-107.

Fiering, Myron B., Stream-flow Synthesis, Cambridge, Massachusetts, 1967.

Gumbel, E. J., Statistics of Extremes, New York: Columbia University Press, 1958.

Hirschleifer, Jack, "On the Theory of Optimal Investment Decisions," Journal of Political Economy, 66, 1958, pp. 329-352.

Hirschleifer, Jack, Disaster and Recovery: A Historical Survey, RAND Memo, RM-3079-PR, April, 1963.

Homan, A. G. and Bruce Waybur, A Study of Procedure in Estimating Flood Damage to Residential, Commercial, and Industrial Properties in California, Menlo Park, California: Stanford Research Institute, 1960.

Howard, Ronald A., Dynamic Programming and Markov Processes, Cambridge: M. I. T. Press, 1960.

Hoyt, William G. and Walter B. Langbein, Floods, Princeton: Princeton University Press, 1954.

Hufschmidt, Maynard M. and Myron B. Fiering, Simulation Techniques for Design of Water-Resource Systems, Cambridge, Massachusetts, 1966.

Jorgenson, D. W., J. J. McCall, and R. Radner, Optimal Replacement Policy, Chicago: Rand-McNally; Amsterdam: North-Holland, 1967.

Kates, Robert William, Hazard and Choice Perception in Flood Plain Management, Department of Geography, Research Paper No. 78, Chicago: University of Chicago Press, 1962.

Koopmans, Tjalling C., Three Essays on the State of Economic Science, New York: McGraw-Hill, 1957.

Koopmans, Tjalling C., "Stationary Ordinal Utility and Impatience," Econometrica, 1960, 287-309.

Krutilla, John V., "An Economic Approach to Coping with Flood Damage," Water Resources Research, II, Second Quarter, 1966, 183-90.

Krutilla, J. V. and Otto Eckstein, Multiple Purpose River Development, Baltimore: Johns Hopkins Press, 1958.

Loucks, Daniel P., et. al., Stochastic Methods for Analyzing River Basin Systems, Cornell University, Water Resources and Marine Sciences Center, Technical Report No. 16, August, 1969.

Luce, R. Duncan and Howard Raiffa, Games and Decisions: Introduction and Critical Survey, New York: John Wiley and Sons, 1957.

Maass, Arthur, Maynard Hufschmidt, Robert Dorfman, Harold A. Thomas, Jr., Stephen A. Marglin, Gordon M. Fair, Design of Water-Resource Systems, Cambridge, Massachusetts: Harvard University Press, 1962.

Manne, Alan S., "Linear Programming and Sequential Decisions," Management Science, April, 1960, 259-267.

Marglin, S., "The Opportunity Cost of Public Investment," Quarterly Journal of Economics, LXXVII, May, 1963.

McCall, John J., "Maintenance Policies for Stochastically Failing Equipment: A Survey," Management Science, 11, 5, March, 1965.

Morey, Richard C., "Some Stochastic Properties of a Compound Renewal Damage Model," Operations Research, September-October, 1966, pp. 902-908.

Parikh, S. C., "Generalized Stochastic Programs with Deterministic Recourse," Master's Thesis, University of California, Berkeley, 1967.

Pendleton, William C., "The Economics of Flood Plain Land Use Regulation," unpublished manuscript, 1967.

Raiffa, Howard, Decision Analysis: Introductory Lectures on Choices Under Uncertainty, Reading, Massachusetts: Addison-Wesley, 1968.

Raiffa, Howard and Robert Schlaifer, Applied Statistical Decision Theory, Boston: Harvard Business School, 1961.

Ramsey, Frank P., "Truth and Probability," (1926), reprinted in The Foundation of Mathematics and Other Logical Essays, Paterson, New Jersey: Littlefield, Adams, & Co., 1960.

Savage, Leonard J., The Foundations of Statistics, New York: John Wiley and Sons, 1954.

Scheaffer, John Richard, Flood Proofing: An Element in a Flood Damage Reduction Program, Department of Geography, Research Paper No. 65, Chicago: University of Chicago Press, 1960.

Smith, Vernon L., "Depreciation, Market Valuations, and Investment Theory," Management Science, 9, 4, July, 1963, pp. 690-96.

Strotz, Robert H., "The Use of Land Rent Charges to Measure the Welfare Benefits of Land Improvement," Manuscript submitted to Resources for the Future, Inc., July, 1966 (Preliminary draft).

United States Army, Corps of Engineers, Engineer District, San Francisco, California, Economic Impact Study of December, 1964 Floods in Northern California Coastal Streams, San Francisco, 1967.

United States Army, Corps of Engineers, Engineer District, San Francisco, California, Report on Floods of December, 1964 in Northern California Coastal Streams, in three volumes, San Francisco, 1965.

U. S. Congress, House, Public Works Committee, Disaster Relief Act of 1965, Hearings, 89th Congress, First Session, Parts I and II, 1965.

U. S. Congress, House, Study of Federal Financial Assistance to Natural Disaster Victims, Report of the House Committee on Banking and Currency, 89th Congress, First Session, H. Rept. 632, 1965.

U. S. Congress, House, Unified National Program for Managing Flood Losses: Report of the Task Force on Federal Flood Control Policy, House Document, 89th Congress, No. 465, 1966.

U. S. Congress, Senate, Federal Disaster Insurance, Report of the Committee on Banking and Currency, 84th Congress, Second Session, Senate Report No. 1313, 1956.

U. S. Congress, Senate, Banking and Currency Committee, Insurance and Other Programs for Financial Assistance to Flood Victims, 89th Congress, Second Session, 1966.

U. S. Congress, Senate, Policies, Standards, and Procedures in the Formulation, Evaluation, and Review of Plans for Use and Development of Water and Related Land Resources, Report by the President's Water Resources Council, 87th Congress, Second Session, S. Doc. No. 97, May 29, 1952.

United States Inter-Agency Committee on Water Resources, Subcommittee on Evaluation Standards, Proposed Practices for Economic Analysis of River Basin Projects, Revised Report, Washington, D. C., May, 1958.

United States Water Resources Council, "A Uniform Technique for Determining Flood Flow Frequencies," 1025 Vermont Avenue, N.W., Washington, D.C., 1967.

University of California, Agricultural Extension Service, An Economic and Water Use Study for Nine Northeastern California Counties, Redding, California, Northern California County Supervisors Association, 1964.

Van Dantzig, D., "Economic Decision Problems of Flood Prevention," Econometrica, 24, 3, July, 1956.

Von Neumann, John, and Oskar Morgenstern, The Theory of Games and Economic Behavior, Second Edition, Princeton, New Jersey: Princeton University Press, 1947.

White, Gilbert F., et. al., Changes in Urban Occupance of Flood Plains in the United States, Department of Geography, Research Paper No. 57, Chicago: University of Chicago Press, 1958.

White, Gilbert F. (ed.), <u>Papers on Flood Problems</u>, Department of Geography, Research Paper No. 70, Chicago: University of Chicago Press, 1961.

White, Gilbert F., <u>Choice of Adjustment to Floods</u>, Department of Geography, Research Paper No. 93, Chicago: University of Chicago Press, 1964.

```
FILE: PRINT    SYSIN    P1                    BROWN UNIVERSITY COMPUTING LABORATORY

C        SIMULATION OFASSIGNMENT OF ACTIVITIES TO LAND IN A FLOOD PLAIN
C      A=INITIAL COST OF ACTIVITY
C      AGE=REPLACEMENT O INTERVAL IF NO FLOOD
C     ALLEPV     ACCUMULATION OF EXPECTED PRESENT VALUES  (CONDITIONAL)
C    AMAX    VALUE OF OPTIMAL ACTIVITY  FOR GIVIEN ZMU
C     AMESS     INTERMEDIATE VARIABLE IN CALCULATION CF OF VDRY
C        B      BENEFIT RATE FOR A ACTIVITY
C     BPROD    INTERMEDIATE VARIBLE IN CALC OF  W
C     DELTA     EXPONENTIAL RATE OF DECAY OF CAPITAL
C     EPV   EXPECTED PRESENT VALUE
C        EPVBAR    AVERAGE EXPECTED PRESENT VALUE  ( CONDITIONAL)
C     EPVUNC     UNCONDITIONAL EXPECTED PRESENT VALUE
C     FLINT   FLOOD INTERVAL
C     FLINTL    INTERVAL UNTIL NEXT FLOOD  NOT NECESSARILY SINCE LAST
C     FLIP   COUNTER (ZERO-ONE) FOR IF FLOOD COMES AFTER TIME HORIZON
C     I      COUNTER FOR NUMBER OF SAMPLES OF ZMU CRAWN
C     ISTOP     NUMBER OF SAMPLES OF ZMU TO BE DRAWN IN PROBLEM
C     IT     INTERMEDIATE VARIABLE IN MAKING TABLE
C      IX    START FOR RANDU RANDOM NUMBER GENERZTOR
C      IY      NEW VALUE IN RANDOM NUMBER GENERATCR
C      J     COUNTER FOR NUMBER OF HISTORIES IN EACH SAMPLE VALUE FOR ZMU
C     JR   PARAMETER OF PRIOR DS
C     JR   PARAMETER OF PRIOR DISTRIBUTION = NO. OF FLOODS OBSERVED
C      JSTOP   NO OF HISTORIES TO BE DONE IN EACH SAMPLE
C     JRZERO   INITIAL VALUE OF JR
C      MAXACT     NUMBER OF OPTIMAL ACTIVITY FOR GIVEN ZMU
C     MINT  INTERMEDIATE VARIABLE INCALCULATING TABLE OF V'S AND VTILDES
C     N    COUNTER FOR ACTIVITY NUMBER
C     NBUYER     INTEGER. THE FIRST @NBUYER@ACTIVITIES ARE TERMINAL SALES
C     NSTOP   NUMBER OF ACTIVITIES TO BE CONSIDERED
C     PV     PRESENT VALUE
C     PVBAR     AVERAGE PRESENT VALUE
C     RANDUM     INTERMEDIATE VALUE TAKEN BY RANCOM NUMBER
C     RETURN     EXPECTED RETURN PERICD FOR FLOOD  =1.0/ZMU
C     RHO    CONTINUOUS DISCOUNT RATE
C    SUMPV     SUM OF PRESINT VALUES  SO FAR IN SAMPLE
C     T     PARAMETER OF PRIOR DISTRIBUTION   TIME PROCESS OBSERVED
C     TAB    TABLE OF VALUES OF ACTIVITIES AS FUNCTION OF MU
C     TCAL     CALENDAR TIME
C     TEMP   TEMPORARY VBLE IN CALCULATION OF VDRY
```

```
FILE: PRINT    SYSIN    P1                        BROWN UNIVERSITY COMPUTING LABORATORY
C     TFLOOD      CALENDAR TIME OF NEXT FLOOD
C     TSTOP      LENGTH OF EACH HISTORY    (TIME HORIZON)
C     TZERO      INITIAL VALUE OF T
C     V     NECESSARY FOR CALLING TOPACT (VALUE OF ACTIVITY AT ZMU)
C     VCHEK  =V
C     VDRY      VALUE GENERATED BY ACTIVITY UNTIL AGE, I.E. NO FLOOD
C      VTRUE   THE EXPECTED PRESENT VALUE OF ACTIVITY BASED ON TRUE MU
C     W      VALUE GENERATED BY ACTIVITY UNTIL NEXT FLOOD (BEFORE AGE)
C     ZMU      VALUE OF INTENSITY PARAMETER OF FLOOD PROCESS --MU
C     ZMUHAT      ESTIMATE OF MU
C     ZMUNEW    INITIAL VALUE OF ZMUHAT
C     ZMUT NEW NAME FOR ZMU (USED IN SEPARATE CALCULATION)
C
C     SUBPROGRAMS CALLED BY MAIN PROGRAM: RANDU,TOPACT,EXP,PLOT,ALOG,VALUE,
C                                          GAMMA.

C  N.B. DIMENSION CHANGE REQUIRES CHANGE IN DECISION PROCESS AND NSTOP
      DIMENSION A( 5),B( 5),AGE( 5),DELTA( 5),VDRY( 5),V(5),VTRUE( 5)
      DIMENSION VCHEK(5)
      DIMENSION TAB(100,6)
C          INPUT FORMAT
  349 FORMAT (I10)
  350 FORMAT(I10,3F10.6,3I10)
  351 FORMAT (4F10.6)
  352 FORMAT (I10)
C          OUTPUT FORMAT
  238 FORMAT ('1   JRZERO     TZERO       RHO      TSTOP      NSTOP      IS
     1TOP       JSTOP'/I10,3F10.4,3I10)
  239 FORMAT ('           A          B        AGE      DELTA'/4F10.4)
  241 FORMAT (' INITIAL EXPECTATION OF ZMU'F10.4,'WITH RETURN PERIOD'
     1F10.4)
  242 FORMAT (I8,F12.3)
  247 FORMAT (' PVBAR='F10.4)
  249 FORMAT (1H ,'SAMPLE OVER. EXPECTED P.V.IS'F13.3,'   CONDITIONAL ON
     1ZMU='F10.4,'      MEAN OVER SAMPLES SO FAR IS',F10.4)
  250 FORMAT (1H,'SAMPLE,HISTORY     TRUE MU')
  251 FORMAT (1H-,9X'UNCONDITIONAL EXPECTED PRESENT VALUE(EPVUNC) IS'
     1F14.4,'BASED ON'I10,'HISTORIES EACH FOR'I10,'VALUES OF ZMU')
  252 FORMAT (2I7, F12.4)
  253 FORMAT ( 1H, F12.4, F10.3, I5,F10.2, 10X,F10.2,10X,I5,F10.3)
```

```
FILE: PRINT     SYSIN     P1
  254 FORMAT ( 1H, F12.4, F10.3, I5,10X,2F10.2,10X,I5,F10.3)
  255 FORMAT (1H,'MU ESTIMATE     DATE ACT;REWARD-DRY;    -FLOOD; VALUE S
     1O FAR')
  257 FORMAT ( 1H, F12.4, F10.3, I5,'  SOLD FOR',2F10.2,10X,I5,F10.3)
  258 FORMAT (' THE FIRST'I10,'ACTIVITIES ARE BY SALE ONLY.')
  259 FORMAT (1H, I10,3F10.3)
  279 FORMAT ('        MU        RETURN       V(1)       V(2)       V(3)
     1V(4)        V(5)       VMAX      MAXACT')
  280 FORMAT (8F10.3,I5)
      READ 349, IX
      READ 350, JRZERO,TZERO,RHO,TSTOP,NSTOP,ISTOP,JSTOP
      READ 351,(A(I),B(I),AGE(I),DELTA(I),I=1,NSTOP)
      PRINT 238, JRZERO,TZERO,RHO,TSTOP,NSTOP,ISTOP,JSTOP
      PRINT 239,(A(I),B(I),AGE(I),DELTA(I),I=1,NSTOP)
      PRINT 258, NBUYER
      PRINT 279
      DO 25 MINT=1,100
      RETURN=MINT
      ZMUT=1./RETURN
      CALL TOPACT(RHO,ZMUT   ,NSTOP,A,B,AGE,DELTA,VCHEK,AMAX,MAXACT)
      PRINT 280,ZMUT,RETURN,VCHEK(1),VCHEK(2),VCHEK(3),VCHEK(4),VCHEK(5)
     1,AMAX,MAXACT
      DO 999 IT=1,5
  999 TAB(MINT,IT+1)=VCHEK(IT)
      TAB(MINT,1)=RETURN
   25 CONTINUE
      CALL PLOT(1,TAB,100,6,100,1)
C        CALCULATE V,VDRY--PRINT V
      ZMUNEW=JRZERO/TZERO
      RETURN=1.0/ZMUNEW

      DO 21 N=1,NSTOP
      TEMP=-RHO*AGE(N)
      AMESS=(1.0-EXP(TEMP))/RHO
      VDRY(N)=-A(N)+B(N)*AMESS
      V(N)=VALUE(A(N),B(N),AGE(N),DELTA(N),RHO,ZMUNEW)
   21 CONTINUE
      PRINT 241,ZMUNEW,RETURN
C           INITIAL CONDITIONS FOR I LOOP--SAMPLES OF ZMU
      ALLEPV=0
      DO 23 I=1,ISTOP
```

```
FILE: PRINT     SYSIN     P1
C          INITIAL CONDITIONS FOR J LOOP --HISTORIES
      SUMPV=0
      CALL GAMMA (JRZERO,TZERO,ZMU)
      DO 22 J=1,JSTOP
C          INITIAL CONDITIONS FOR HISTORY J
      JR=JRZERO
      T=TZERO
      TCAL=0
      TFLOOD=0
      PV=0
      FLIP=0
      PRINT 250
      PRINT 252,1,J,ZMU
      PRINT 255
C          HISTORY GENERATION
    3 IF(FLIP.GT.0) GO TO 5
      CALL RANDU (IX,IY,RANDUM)
      IX=IY
      FLINT=(ALOG(RANDUM))/(-ZMU)
    4 TFLOOD=TFLOOD+FLINT
      IF(TFLOOD.LT.TSTOP) GO TO 7
      FLIP=1
      TFLOOD=TSTOP
C          DECISION PROCESS
    7 T=TCAL +TZERO
      ZMUHAT=JR/T
      CALL TOPACT(RHO,ZMUHAT,NSTOP,A,B,AGE,DELTA,V,AMAX,MAXACT)
      N=MAXACT
C          ACCUMULATION PROCEDURE
   12 IF(TFLOOD.LE.(TCAL+AGE(N))) GO TO 99
C          NO FLOOD UP TO RENEWAL
      PV=PV+VDRY(N)*EXP(-RHO*TCAL)
      PRINT 253, ZMUHAT, TCAL, N, VDRY(N), PV
      TCAL=TCAL+AGE(N)
      GO TO 7
C          FLOOD-CAUSED RENEWAL
   99 FLINTL=TFLOOD-TCAL
      BPROD=(1.0-EXP(-RHO*FLINTL))/RHO
      W=-A(N)+B(N)*BPROD
```

```
      PV=PV+W*EXP(-RHO*TCAL)
      PRINT 254, ZMUHAT, TCAL, N,W, PV
      TCAL=TFLOOD
      JR=JR+1
      GO TO 3
C            END OF HISTORY J
    5 SUMPV=SUMPV+PV
      PVBAR=SUMPV/J
   22 CONTINUE
      DO 20 N=1,NSTOP
      VTRUE(N)=VALUE(A(N),B(N),AGE(N),DELTA(N),RHO,ZMU)
   20 CONTINUE
      EPV=SUMPV/JSTOP
      ALLEPV=ALLEPV+EPV
      EPVBAR=ALLEPV/I
      PRINT 249, EPV,ZMU,EPVBAR
   23 CONTINUE
      EPVUNC=ALLEPV/ISTOP
      PRINT 251,EPVUNC,JSTOP,ISTOP
      END
      SUBROUTINE GAMMA(JRZERO,TZERO,ZMU)
C     JJ        COUNTER FOR NO. OF I.I.D.EXPONENTIAL R.V.S
C     UNITRN         VALUE OF UNIFORMLY DISTRIBUTED RANDOM VARIABLE
C      TR       MULTIPLICATIVE ACCUMULATOR
C            GENERATE A RANDOM NUMBER FROM A GAMMA DISTRIBUT9ON
      TR=1.0
      DO 800 JJ=1,JRZERO
      CALL RANDU(IX,IY,UNITRN)
      IX=IY
  800 TR=TR*UNITRN
      ZMU=-ALOG(TR)/TZERO
      RETURN
      END
      FUNCTION VALUE (A,B,AGE,DELTA,RHO,ZMU)
C     VALUE       EXPECTED PRESENT VALUE OF ACTIVITY FOR GIVEN, KNOWN ZMU
C     ANUM,BTOP,BXPO,CBOT,CONST,CTOP,XPON      INTERMEDIATE VARIABLES
      ANUM=RHO+ZMU+DELTA
      CTOP=RHO+ZMU
      XPON=-CTOP*AGE
      CBOT=RHO*(1.0-2.71828**(XPON))
```

```
      CONST=CTOP/CBOT
      BXPO=-ANUM*AGE
      BTOP=1.0-2.71828**(BXPO)
      VALUE =CONST*(-A+B*(BTOP/ANUM))
      RETURN
      END
      SUBROUTINE TOPACT (RHO,ZMU,NSTOP,A,B,AGE,DELTA,V,AMAX,MAXACT)
C     NN       COUNTER FOR NO OF ACTIVITY BEING CALCULATED
C     V      EXPECTED PRESENT VALUE OF ACTIVITY FOR GIVEN ZMU
      DIMENSION A(NSTOP),B(NSTOP),AGE(NSTOP),DELTA(NSTOP),V(NSTOP)
      AMAX=-1000000.
      MAXACT=0
      DO 15 NN=1,NSTOP
      V(NN)=VALUE(A(NN),B(NN),AGE(NN),DELTA(NN),RHO,ZMU)
      IF(V(NN)-AMAX)15,15,20
   20 AMAX=V(NN)
      MAXACT=NN
   15 CONTINUE
      RETURN
      END
```

Lecture Notes in Economics and Mathematical Systems

(Vol. 1–15: Lecture Notes in Operations Research and Mathematical Economics, Vol. 16–59: Lecture Notes in Operations Research and Mathematical Systems)

Vol. 1: H. Bühlmann, H. Loeffel, E. Nievergelt, Einführung in die Theorie und Praxis der Entscheidung bei Unsicherheit. 2. Auflage, IV, 125 Seiten 4°. 1969. DM 16,–

Vol. 2: U. N. Bhat, A Study of the Queueing Systems M/G/1 and GI/M/1. VIII, 78 pages. 4°. 1968. DM 16,–

Vol. 3: A. Strauss, An Introduction to Optimal Control Theory. VI, 153 pages. 4°. 1968. DM 16,–

Vol. 4: Einführung in die Methode Branch and Bound. Herausgegeben von F. Weinberg. VIII, 159 Seiten. 4°. 1968. DM 16,–

Vol. 5: Hyvärinen, Information Theory for Systems Engineers. VIII, 205 pages. 4°. 1968. DM 16,–

Vol. 6: H. P. Künzi, O. Müller, E. Nievergelt, Einführungskursus in die dynamische Programmierung. IV, 103 Seiten. 4°. 1968. DM 16,–

Vol. 7: W. Popp, Einführung in die Theorie der Lagerhaltung. VI, 173 Seiten. 4°. 1968. DM 16,–

Vol. 8: J. Teghem, J. Loris-Teghem, J. P. Lambotte, Modèles d'Attente M/G/1 et GI/M/1 à Arrivées et Services en Groupes. IV, 53 pages. 4°. 1969. DM 16,–

Vol. 9: E. Schultze, Einführung in die mathematischen Grundlagen der Informationstheorie. VI, 116 Seiten. 4°. 1969. DM 16,–

Vol. 10: D. Hochstädter, Stochastische Lagerhaltungsmodelle. VI, 269 Seiten. 4°. 1969. DM 18,–

Vol. 11/12: Mathematical Systems Theory and Economics. Edited by H. W. Kuhn and G. P. Szegö. VIII, IV, 486 pages. 4°. 1969. DM 34,–

Vol. 13: Heuristische Planungsmethoden. Herausgegeben von F. Weinberg und C. A. Zehnder. II, 93 Seiten. 4°. 1969. DM 16,–

Vol. 14: Computing Methods in Optimization Problems. Edited by A. V. Balakrishnan. V, 191 pages. 4°. 1969. DM 16,–

Vol. 15: Economic Models, Estimation and Risk Programming: Essays in Honor of Gerhard Tintner. Edited by K. A. Fox, G. V. L. Narasimham and J. K. Sengupta. VIII, 461 pages. 4°. 1969. DM 24,–

Vol. 16: H. P. Künzi und W. Oettli, Nichtlineare Optimierung: Neuere Verfahren, Bibliographie. IV, 180 Seiten. 4°. 1969. DM 16,–

Vol. 17: H. Bauer und K. Neumann, Berechnung optimaler Steuerungen, Maximumprinzip und dynamische Optimierung. VIII, 188 Seiten. 4°. 1969. DM 16,–

Vol. 18: M. Wolff, Optimale Instandhaltungspolitiken in einfachen Systemen. V, 143 Seiten. 4°. 1970. DM 16,–

Vol. 19: L. Hyvärinen, Mathematical Modeling for Industrial Processes. VI, 122 pages. 4°. 1970. DM 16,–

Vol. 20: G. Uebe, Optimale Fahrpläne. IX, 161 Seiten. 4°. 1970. DM 16,–

Vol. 21: Th. Liebling, Graphentheorie in Planungs- und Tourenproblemen am Beispiel des städtischen Straßendienstes. IX, 118 Seiten. 4°. 1970. DM 16,–

Vol. 22: W. Eichhorn, Theorie der homogenen Produktionsfunktion. VIII, 119 Seiten. 4°. 1970. DM 16,–

Vol. 23: A. Ghosal, Some Aspects of Queueing and Storage Systems. IV, 93 pages. 4°. 1970. DM 16,–

Vol. 24: Feichtinger, Lernprozesse in stochastischen Automaten. V, 66 Seiten. 4°. 1970. DM 16,–

Vol. 25: R. Henn und O. Opitz, Konsum- und Produktionstheorie. I. II, 124 Seiten. 4°. 1970. DM 16,–

Vol. 26: D. Hochstädter und G. Uebe, Ökonometrische Methoden. XII, 250 Seiten. 4°. 1970. DM 18,–

Vol. 27: I. H. Mufti, Computational Methods in Optimal Control Problems. IV, 45 pages. 4°. 1970. DM 16,–

Vol. 28: Theoretical Approaches to Non-Numerical Problem Solving. Edited by R. B. Banerji and M. D. Mesarovic. VI, 466 pages. 4°. 1970. DM 24,–

Vol. 29: S. E. Elmaghraby, Some Network Models in Management Science. III, 177 pages. 4°. 1970. DM 16,–

Vol. 30: H. Noltemeier, Sensitivitätsanalyse bei diskreten linearen Optimierungsproblemen. VI, 102 Seiten. 4°. 1970. DM 16,–

Vol. 31: M. Kühlmeyer, Die nichtzentrale t-Verteilung. II, 106 Seiten. 4°. 1970. DM 16,–

Vol. 32: F. Bartholomes und G. Hotz, Homomorphismen und Reduktionen linearer Sprachen. XII, 143 Seiten. 4°. 1970. DM 16,–

Vol. 33: K. Hinderer, Foundations of Non-stationary Dynamic Programming with Discrete Time Parameter. VI, 160 pages. 4°. 1970. DM 16,–

Vol. 34: H. Störmer, Semi-Markoff-Prozesse mit endlich vielen Zuständen. Theorie und Anwendungen. VII, 128 Seiten. 4°. 1970. DM 16,–

Vol. 35: F. Ferschl, Markovketten. VI, 168 Seiten. 4°. 1970. DM 16,–

Vol. 36: M. P. J. Magill, On a General Economic Theory of Motion. VI, 95 pages. 4°. 1970. DM 16,–

Vol. 37: H. Müller-Merbach, On Round-Off Errors in Linear Programming. VI, 48 pages. 4°. 1970. DM 16,–

Vol. 38: Statistische Methoden I, herausgegeben von E. Walter. VIII, 338 Seiten. 4°. 1970. DM 22,–

Vol. 39: Statistische Methoden II, herausgegeben von E. Walter. IV, 155 Seiten. 4°. 1970. DM 16,–

Vol. 40: H. Drygas, The Coordinate-Free Approach to Gauss-Markov Estimation. VIII, 113 pages. 4°. 1970. DM 16,–

Vol. 41: U. Ueing, Zwei Lösungsmethoden für nichtkonvexe Programmierungsprobleme. VI, 92 Seiten. 4°. 1971. DM 16,–

Vol. 42: A. V. Balakrishnan, Introduction to Optimization Theory in a Hilbert Space. IV, 153 pages. 4°. 1971. DM 16,–

Vol. 43: J. A. Morales, Bayesian Full Information Structural Analysis. VI, 154 pages. 4°. 1971. DM 16,–

Vol. 44: G. Feichtinger, Stochastische Modelle demographischer Prozesse. XIII, 404 pages. 4°. 1971. DM 28,–

Vol. 45: K. Wendler, Hauptaustauschschritte (Principal Pivoting). II, 64 pages. 4°. 1971. DM 16,–

Vol. 46: C. Boucher, Leçons sur la théorie des automates mathématiques. VIII, 193 pages. 4°. 1971. DM 18,–

Vol. 47: H. A. Nour Eldin, Optimierung linearer Regelsysteme mit quadratischer Zielfunktion. VIII, 163 pages. 4°. 1971. DM 16,–

Vol. 48: M. Constam, Fortran für Anfänger. VI, 143 pages. 4°. 1971. DM 16,–

Vol. 49: Ch. Schneeweiß, Regelungstechnische stochastische Optimierungsverfahren. XI, 254 pages. 4°. 1971. DM 22,–

Vol. 50: Unternehmensforschung Heute – Übersichtsvorträge der Züricher Tagung von SVOR und DGU, September 1970. Herausgegeben von M. Beckmann. VI, 133 pages. 4°. 1971. DM 16,–

Vol. 51: Digitale Simulation. Herausgegeben von K. Bauknecht und W. Nef. IV, 207 pages. 4°. 1971. DM 18,–

Vol. 52: Invariant Imbedding. Proceedings of the Summer Workshop on Invariant Imbedding Held at the University of Southern California, June – August 1970. Edited by R. E. Bellman and E. D. Denman. IV, 148 pages. 4°. 1971. DM 16,–

Vol. 53: J. Rosenmüller, Kooperative Spiele und Märkte. IV, 152 pages. 4°. 1971. DM 16,–

Vol. 54: C. C. von Weizsäcker, Steady State Capital Theory. III, 102 pages. 4°. 1971. DM 16,–

Vol. 55: P. A. V. B. Swamy, Statistical Inference in Random Coefficient Regression Models. VIII, 209 pages. 4°. 1971. DM 20,–

Vol. 56: Mohamed A. El-Hodiri, Constrained Extrema. Introduction to the Differentiable Case with Economic Applications. III, 130 pages. 4°. 1971. DM 16,–

Vol. 57: E. Freund, Zeitvariable Mehrgrößensysteme. VII, 160 pages. 4°. 1971. DM 18,–

Vol. 58: P. B. Hagelschuer, Theorie der linearen Dekomposition. VII, 191 pages. 4°. 1971. DM 18,–

Vol. 59: J. A. Hanson, Growth in Open Economics. IV, 127 pages. 4°. 1971. DM 16,–

Vol. 60: H. Hauptmann, Schätz- und Kontrolltheorie in stetigen dynamischen Wirtschaftsmodellen. V, 104 pages. 4°. 1971. DM 16,–

Vol. 61: K. H. F. Meyer, Wartesysteme mit variabler Bearbeitungsrate. VII, 314 pages. 4°. 1971. DM 24,–

Vol. 62: W. Krelle u. G. Gabisch unter Mitarbeit von J. Burgermeister, Wachstumstheorie. VII, 223 pages. 4°. 1972. DM 20,–

Vol. 63: J. Kohlas, Monte Carlo Simulation im Operations Research. VI, 162 pages. 4°. 1972. DM 16,–

Vol. 64: P. Gessner u. K. Spremann, Optimierung in Funktionenräumen. IV, 120 pages. 4°. 1972. DM 16,–.

Vol. 65: W. Everling, Exercises in Computer Systems Analysis. VIII, 184 pages. 4°. 1972. DM 18,–

Vol. 66: F. Bauer, P. Garabedian und D. Korn, Supercritical Wing Sections. V, 211 pages. 4°. 1972. DM 20,–.

Vol. 67: I. V. Girsanov, Lectures on Mathematical Theory of Extremum Problems. V, 136 pages. 4°. 1972. DM 16,–.

Vol. 68: J. Loeckx, Computability and Decidability. An Introduction for Students of Computer Science. VI, 76 pages. 4°. 1972. DM 16,–

Vol. 69: S. Ashour, Sequencing Theory. V, 133 pages. 4°. 1972. DM 16,–.

Vol. 70: J. P. Brown, The Economic Effects of Floods. Investigations of a Stochastic Model of Rational Investment Behavior in the Face of Floods. V, 87 pages. 4°. 1972. DM 16,–.

66 PB